MARTIN & WERNER FEIERSINGER: *ITALOMODERN 1*
ARCHITECTURE IN NORTHERN ITALY 1946–1976

PARK BOOKS

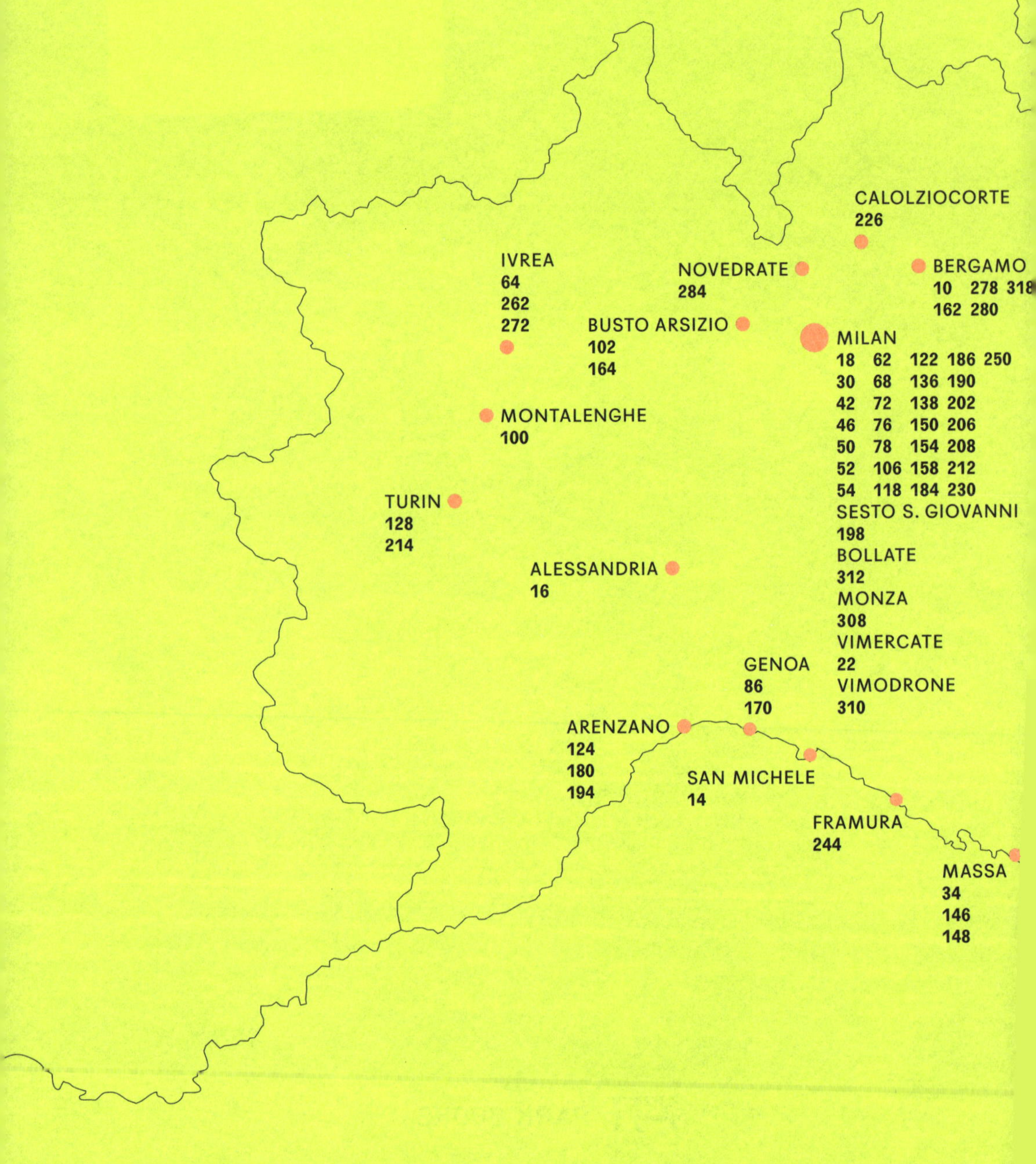
CALOLZIOCORTE
226
IVREA
64
262
272
NOVEDRATE
284
BERGAMO
10 278 318
162 280
BUSTO ARSIZIO
102
164
MILAN
18 62 122 186 250
30 68 136 190
42 72 138 202
46 76 150 206
50 78 154 208
52 106 158 212
54 118 184 230
MONTALENGHE
100
TURIN
128
214
SESTO S. GIOVANNI
198
ALESSANDRIA
16
BOLLATE
312
MONZA
308
VIMERCATE
22
GENOA
86
170
VIMODRONE
310
ARENZANO
124
180
194
SAN MICHELE
14
FRAMURA
244
MASSA
34
146
148

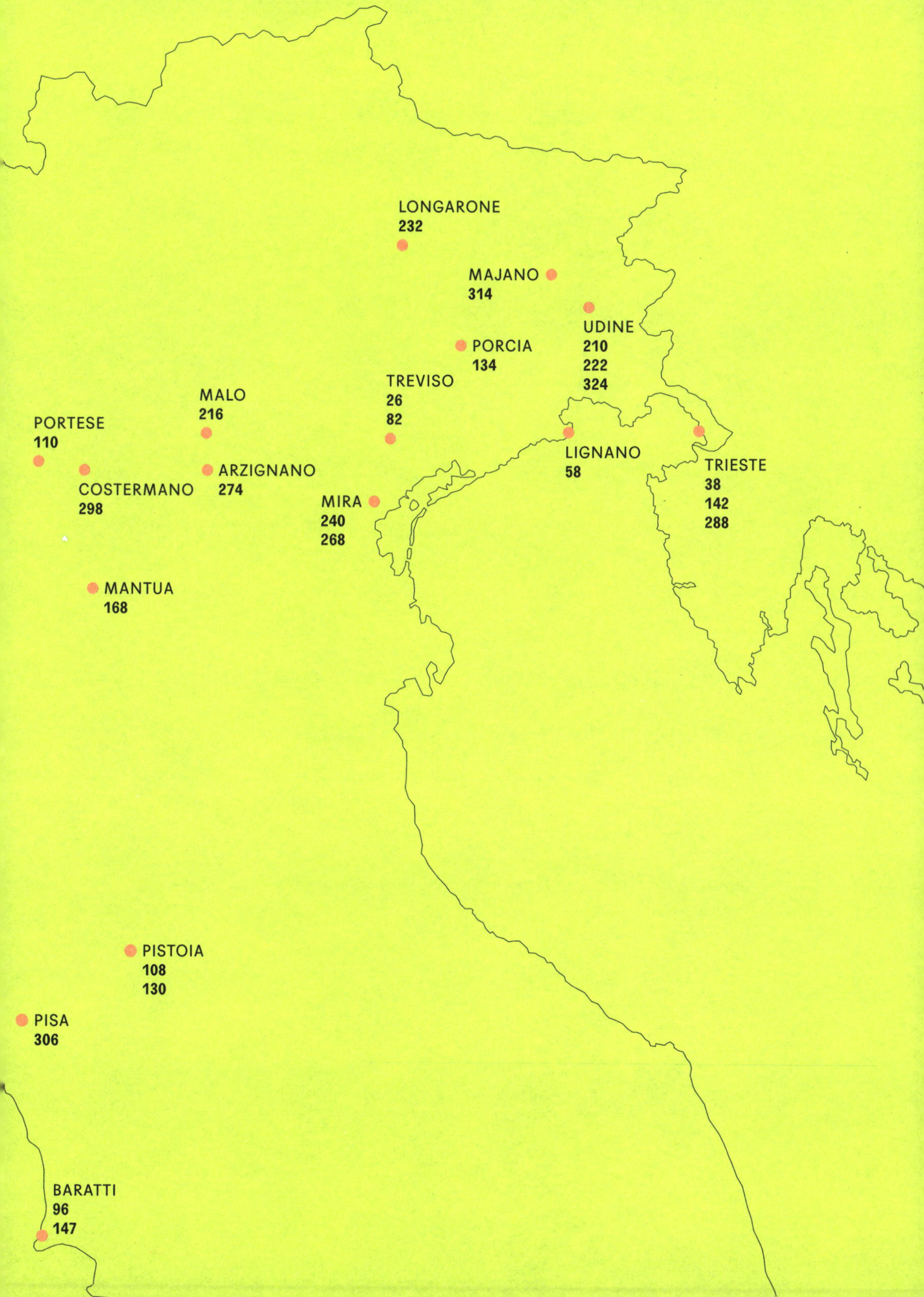
LONGARONE
232
MAJANO
314
UDINE
210
222
324
PORCIA
134
TREVISO
26
82
MALO
216
PORTESE
110
ARZIGNANO
274
COSTERMANO
298
LIGNANO
58
TRIESTE
38
142
288
MIRA
240
268
MANTUA
168
PISTOIA
108
130
PISA
306
BARATTI
96
147

ARNO RITTER: *A LOGBOOK*

Compelling projects often originate from coincidences. The starting point of Martin and Werner Feiersinger's project was a pragmatic circumstance in the year 2004. Concluding a study trip to several of Le Corbusier's buildings in France, they made their way home via Milan in order to have a look at the Mater Misericordiae church by Angelo Mangiarotti and Bruno Morassutti. After the rather sculptural structures of Corbu, which were of particular interest to the sculptor and photographer Werner Feiersinger, they experienced the comparatively "sober" sacral space by Mangiarotti & Morassutti, designed according to constructive and conceptual considerations, as a certain counterpoint to what they had just seen in France. It was probably the combination of various aspects—on the one hand, the fascination with the "charged space"; on the other hand, Martin's architecturally trained eye, and, ultimately, the keen desire to physically experience buildings in their present-day environments—which led to a passion that continues to this day and is now presented for the first time in this book.

Ensuing from comprehensive research in books and magazines from the nineteen-forties to nineteen-sixties, the two of them regularly tour northern Italy, where striking, unconventional buildings arose after the Second World War. It is not only the so-called second classic modern period that interests Martin and Werner, but also the structures that express the economic and cultural upsurge in Italy in which there was still the conviction—though it might seem naive today—that architecture could shape the future and society.

The focus lies on singular, ambivalent manifestations, on experimental, though not necessarily spectacular, architectures that they seek out and document. In doing so, they trace the biographies of individual architects, discover how architects influence each other, but also explore structural interrelations and penetrate in a certain sense into the sociotope of that postwar era. Consequently, over the years, an extensive collection of material has emerged—a phenomenology of the heterogeneous, unique in its ambiguity and ambivalence.

For Martin and Werner Feiersinger, however, it is not a matter of a strictly scholarly review of this stylistic pluralism in postwar Italy. Proceeding from their distinct ways of working, in their survey they attempt to make visible the different qualities of the individual structures—independent of the current condition of the building. "Our emphasis is twofold, corresponding to our perspectives as a sculptor and as an architect: on the one hand, it has to do with the sculptural qualities of the buildings, the materiality, and the various surfaces, and, on the other hand, with the shaping of space, the functional conception, and the integration into the surroundings."

In this project, Martin takes over the role of the explorer and collector. His considerable knowledge, down to the smallest biographical and architectural details, is based on his ever-growing library, as well as a slip box that has, over the years, become a true treasure trove. While he re-examines the groundwork, makes the selection of the buildings and brings his architectural eye to the project, Werner reacts to the buildings in a subjective and unbiased manner as an artist and a photographer.

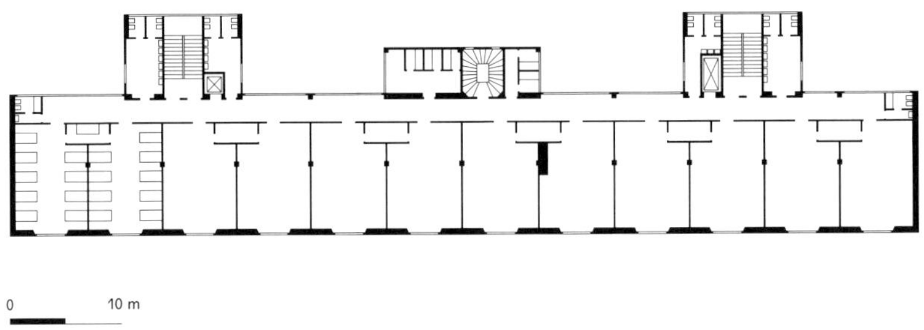

1948–54

LUIGI CACCIA DOMINIONI

CONVENTO E ISTITUTO DELLA BEATA VERGINE ADDOLORATA
MILAN, VIA CALATAFIMI 10

The main facade of this Catholic orphanage has a structure similar to the house on Piazza Sant'Ambrogio that, beginning in 1947, Caccia Dominioni built for his own family. Situated above the ground floor is the *piano nobile* with colonnade. Then there are two simple, unembellished levels. At the very top, a loggia runs the entire length of the facade. While the design of the architect's own residence is a reinterpretation of a palazzo that had been destroyed in the war, the orphanage is less formal. Here Caccia Dominioni adopted an element from agricultural structures: he integrated into the building's elegant skin the brick grilles that appear in the region's barns. This was the first in a long line of facades clad in ceramic tile: over the course of his career, Caccia Dominioni employed them in a variety of colors and formats.

10
ASILO NIDO

1948–60

LUIGI CACCIA DOMINIONI, LIVIO CASTIGLIONI, PIER GIACOMO CASTIGLIONI

SCHOOL

VIMERCATE, PIAZZALE MARTIRI VIMERCATESI

After receiving his architecture degree, Luigi Caccia Dominioni initially worked with the Castiglioni brothers. Together they submitted proposals to several competitions, including a design for a school in Vimercate. Situated in front of the main school building, the aula magna is the crux of the design: it is an asymmetrical, bold structure whose north elevation is made of translucent glass blocks. The side walls, like the outer envelope of the nearby school wings, are clad in tile. In contrast, all parts of the building oriented toward the schoolyard have simple stucco facades.

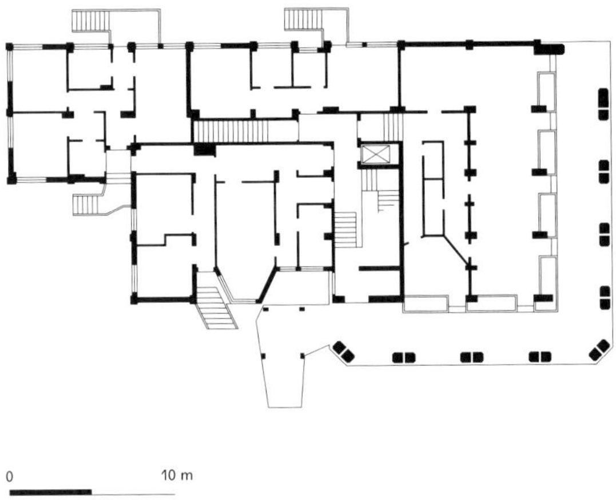

1949–53

GIUSEPPE SAMONÀ

MIXED-USE BUILDING
TREVISO, VIA ROMA, LARGO PORTA ALTINIA 23

This building has a tripartite organization. The six-story block on Via Roma has a planar facade, while the block behind it has a stepped cross-section and balconies parallel to the city's old fortification wall. A shift in scale comes into view on the side facing Largo Porta Altinia. Here the building massing is more finely apportioned, and the block is considerably smaller, as if it were a single-family house with all the trappings, including a front yard and its own entrance, yet attached to the main building. In the area between the higher and lower blocks, a slender marquee roof points the way to a colonnade of bulky, paired columns. In addition to the treatment of the building massing, Samonà was interested in "frame and infill." The structural framework is clearly legible.

INA
CM 117FR
CP 332MX

CAFFE
barVENEZIA

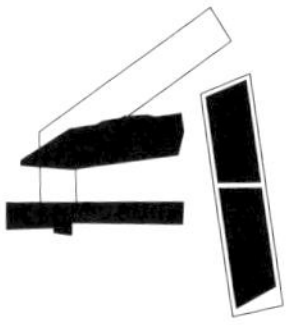

M 1:5000

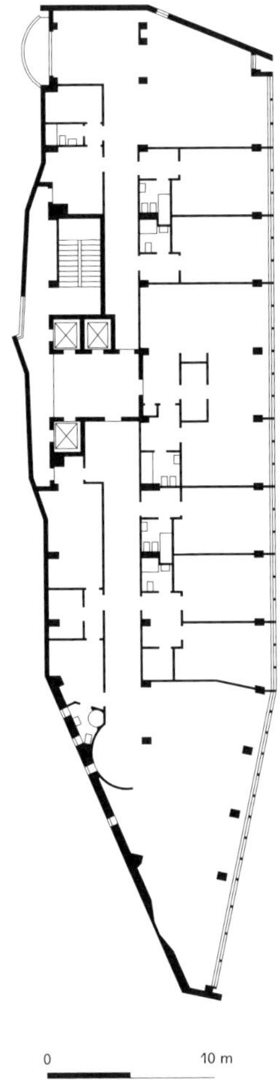

1949–56

LUIGI MORETTI

MIXED-USE BUILDING

MILAN, CORSO ITALIA 13, VIA RUGABELLA

For this project, Luigi Moretti acted both as architect and as investor. The multi-faceted complex stands in marked contrast to its surroundings. Along Corso Italia the building massing tapers expressively: a wedge-shaped wing is situated perpendicular to the street, interrupting the frontage. This makes it possible to discern the different parts as distinct entities. On top of that, by opening toward the street the thrust of its space is altered. The treatment of the rear residential wing's massing is in the same vein: a narrow slit cuts the fourteen-story residential high-rise in two parts. In the striking, wedge-shaped wing there are three apartments per story. The space where the walls converge contains a large living room.

RISTORANTE
Banco del Gusto
PROPRIETÀ PRIVATA

RISTORANTE

CUSHMAN & WAKEFIELD
AFFITTASI UFFICI
02 637991

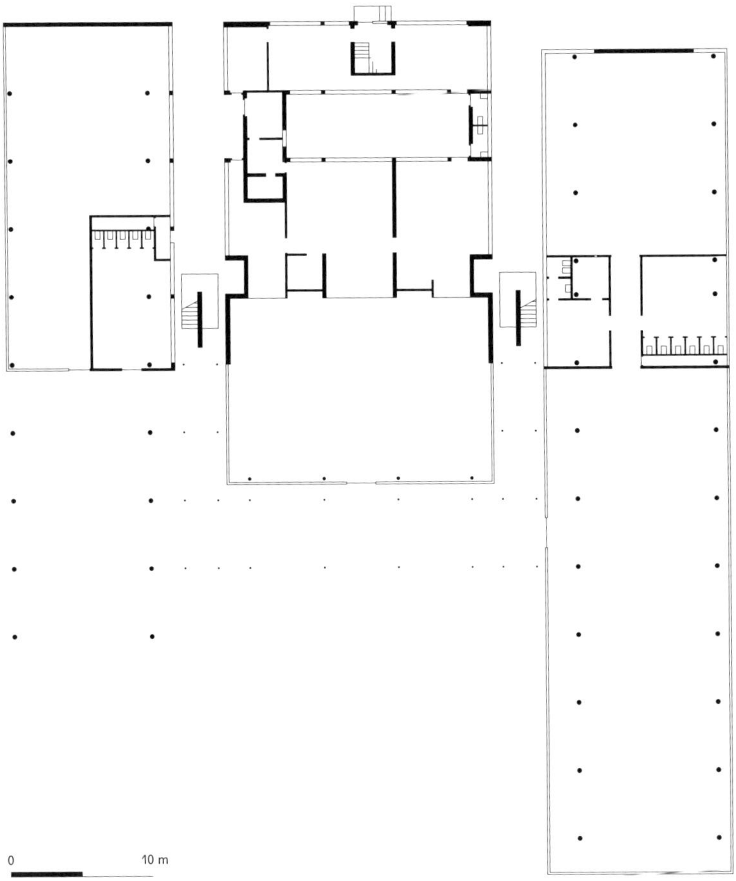

1950–56

ANNIBALE FIOCCHI

OLIVETTI SUMMER CAMP
MARINA DI MASSA, VIA BONDANO 51

Olivetti erected this summer camp for its employees' children. It was the last such camp to be built in Marina di Massa and is much smaller than those dating to the nineteen-thirties. The building was planned for 120 children, while the neighboring facility, designed by Ettore Sottsass Sr., accommodates 1000 children. The aims so often pursued by architects—lightness, airiness, and transparency—are indeed achieved here: the play areas on the ground floor are completely glazed, and the columns are so slender that they could be mistaken for piping. On the upper level an ambulatory runs along the outer edges of the dormitories. The staircases are open to the elements. The camp's infirmary [→37] has a slightly modified formal vocabulary. In the photo, the single-story structure is in the foreground; a Sottsass building is right behind it.

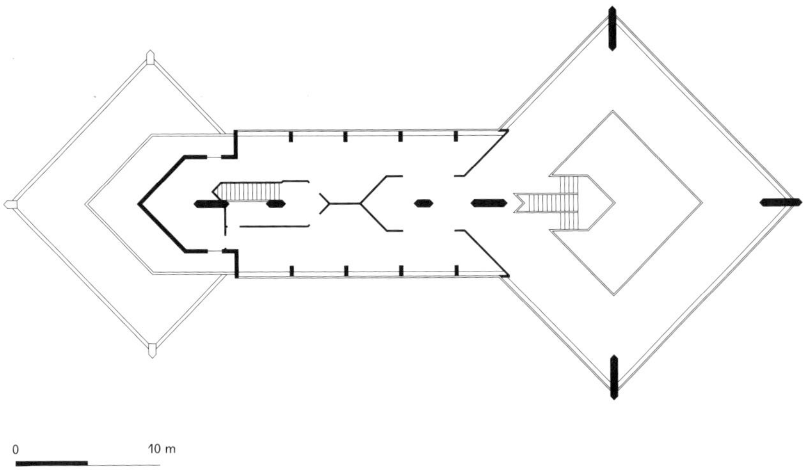

MARCELLO D'OLIVO

VILLAGGIO DEL FANCIULLO, CAFETERIA
TRIESTE, OPICINA, VIA DI CONCONELLO 16

1950–57

The children's village outside Trieste is made up of a number of buildings designed by Marcello D'Olivo. These include a school and accompanying preschool, three dormitories, a workshop building and a printing shop. The main building, which is clearly influenced by the work of Frank Lloyd Wright, holds the cafeteria. Immediately following its completion, the cafeteria was deemed one of the prime examples of *Tendenza organica*. The floor plan consists of two squares positioned on their vertices and a narrow linking element that connects them on the diagonal. The resulting 45° angle became the determinant formal element: it was implemented even at the finest level of detail, for example, in the design of the handrails. Both inside and outside, the tilt of the walls underscores the striking geometrical forms.

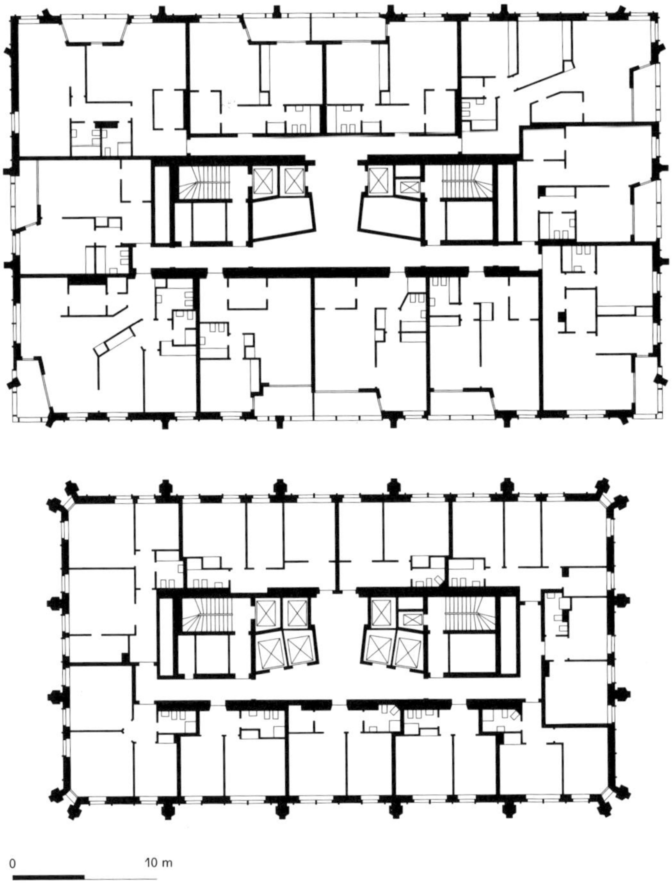

BBPR – LODOVICO BARBIANO DI BELGIOJOSO, ENRICO PERESSUTTI, ERNESTO NATHAN ROGERS

TORRE VELASCA
MILAN, PIAZZA VELASCA 5

1950–58

Ignazio Gardella, a key figure of the "School of Milan," made an unusual declaration: he said that he wished Torre Velasca were his design—even though from the very beginning the skyscraper in downtown Milan was a controversial undertaking. Its formal vocabulary contrasts strongly with the consensus of the day—in particular, with skyscrapers built in International Style. Instead of insisting on an ethereal, sheer look, BBPR topped the tower's distinctive silhouette with a sloped copper roof; instead of a smooth, curtain-wall facade, there are discrete, freely arranged windows. The narrower part of the tower contains offices and apartments. From the nineteenth story upward, where the floor area is larger, it contains apartments.

Brunelleschi
Hotel
POPOLARE
70
DP 084SS
80

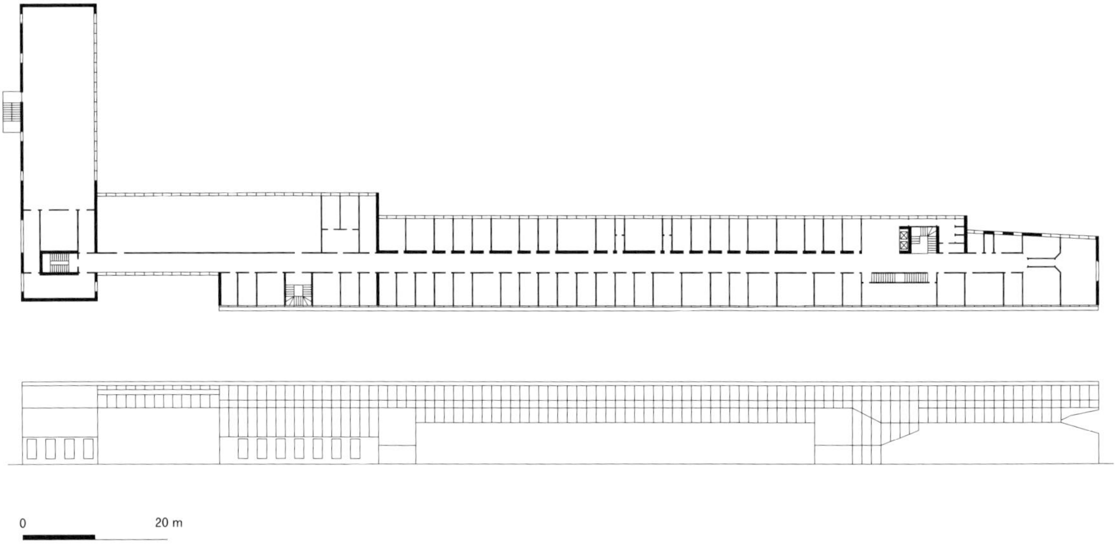

1951–57

LUIGI CACCIA DOMINIONI

LORO & PARISINI OFFICE BUILDING
MILAN, VIA SAVONA 129, VIA FILIPPO BRUNELLESCHI

Caccia Dominioni's design oscillates between tradition and modernity: he takes cues from rural utilitarian architecture as well as from modular industrial construction. A tiled, nearly windowless base holds storage rooms and supports the crystalline office level sheathed in a curtain-wall facade. On Via Brunelleschi, the two parts of the building separate: the base metamorphoses into a shed with a roof of its own, and the office level presses on like a sled, presenting a facade with a pitched roof and a single square window. The mixture of playfulness and seriousness makes this part of the building look like an ordinary house floating in the air. Renovation work took place after the photos were shot, but without any sensitivity to Caccia Dominioni's intentions: the dark brown tiles were removed and the surface was refinished in white stucco.

impresa costruzioni edili
fantin

SAMSUNG
immagina di vivere Ultra.
Ultra
SAMSUNG
telena

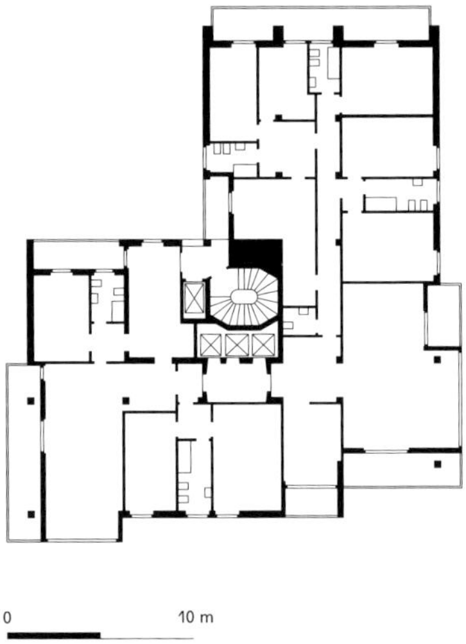

1953–56

VICO MAGISTRETTI

TORRE AL PARCO
MILAN, VIA GIUSEPPE REVERE

Although Magistretti had already realized a number of projects—primarily subsidized housing for *INA-Casa*—he referred to this residential tower on a prominent site near Parco Sempione as his first building. In a design that stacks up twenty-one levels, he—like Caccia Dominioni—explores a new interpretation of apartments for the urban bourgeoisie. Here he opted for two large units per floor—each with multiple balconies and a separate entrance for the household staff. Magistretti also turned his attention to parts of the building that are often neglected, such as the encasement of the elevator's machine room and other building services spaces: the latter are housed in a structure with a tunnel-shaped top. An exterior spiral staircase adjoining the uppermost level provides access to the roof.

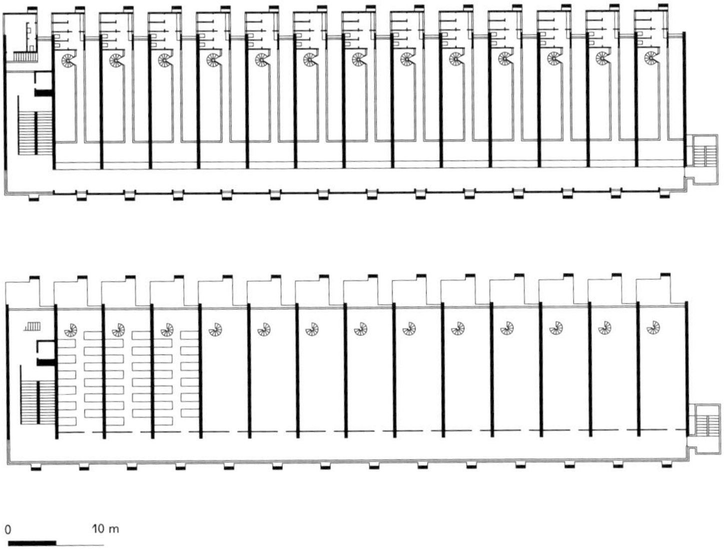

1953–59

VITTORIANO VIGANÒ

ISTITUTO MARCHIONDI

MILAN, VIA NOALE 1

The Istituto Marchiondi is considered Italy's most important brutalist building. It was built as a boarding school for boys with behavioral problems. The complex is made up of a series of single-story structures, a three-story school, and the six-story dormitory. The latter's rooms are double height. Spiral staircases and narrow catwalks that pass through the centers of the rooms lead to the bathrooms, which project from the facade. In keeping with brutalist tenets, all building components are in rough-shuttered reinforced concrete. The concrete piers are set apart from the building massing. The detailing of the roof beams is inspired by timber construction.

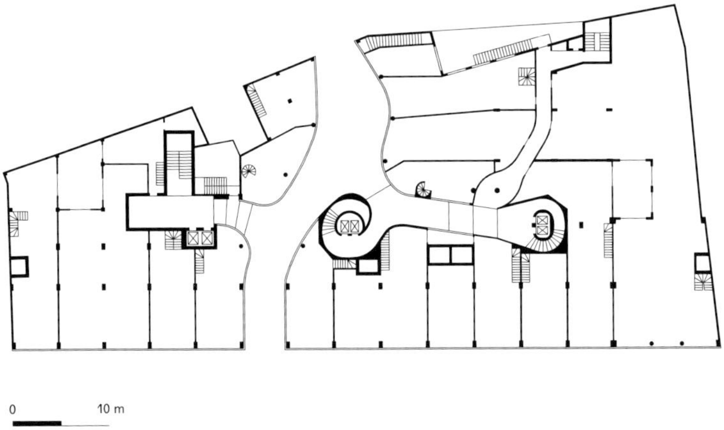

1953–59

LUIGI CACCIA DOMINIONI

MIXED-USE BUILDINGS

MILAN, CORSO EUROPA 10–12 AND 18–20

The two identical office buildings on Corso Europa are reminiscent of Mies van der Rohe's work in Chicago. It is Caccia Dominioni's most rigorous and, in its formal vocabulary, modern project—his interpretation, so to speak, of the International Style. The tiled facade, a recurring theme in his oeuvre, is limited to the transverse elevation on Via Cavallotti. The sinuous passageway reveals the architect's passion for designing floor plans. In an interview he said that he hurls himself into a floor plan as vehemently as the skiers Gustav Thöni and Ingemar Stenmark attack the slalom course.

60 CENTRALE FS
6217
DR 305TS

OTTO KAPFINGER: *ATLANTIS REVISITED*

FIRST NOTE

This book tells, primarily in pictures, the history of contemporary architecture from the perspective of "dilettants"—if we use the word in Egon Friedell's ennobled sense. It is the excerpt-like, photographic-artistic record, the trail of a *recherche sentimentale*, the outcome of a decade-long fascination and obsession pursued by an architect and an artist. It is the documentation of their literally off-center, "eccentric" expeditions—without a commission" and "without systematization"—through the architectural and design-cultural cosmos that arose in northern Italy after 1945, and over the course of the next three decades, swelled to a "panaromatic" heyday and then, comparable to the legendary Atlantis, disappeared overnight from the orbit of regional and global recognition and activity.

What is noteworthy today and has an electrifying effect on us, is, on the one hand, this way of observing, this way of seeing, this unacademic, aesthetic reading of an era already a part of the past, and the act of picturing the building in one's mind's eye. And on the other hand, it is precisely this re-examination that, with the temporal and personal distance, makes visible for us today those (vis-à-vis the present situation both globally and regionally) irritatingly multi-layered, undogmatic and charged, everyday qualities that lift these works of architecture and the period in which they originated out of pure nostalgia and into the intellectual and artistic virulence—as inspiration, as a benchmark in the best sense, both provocative and instructive.

EGON FRIEDELL: *A CULTURAL HISTORY OF THE MODERN AGE*, VOLUME 1. NEW BRUNSWICK 2008 (NEW YORK 1930), P. 15
All our utterances about the past refer equally to ourselves. We can never speak of and never know anything except ourselves. But by sinking ourselves in the past we discover new possibilities of our own ego, enlarge the frontiers of our consciousness, and undergo new if wholly subjective experiences. Therein lies the value and the aim of all historical study.

FRIEDELL: OP. CIT., P. 41
As regards dilettantism, it should be borne in mind that vital energy dwells in any activities only so long as they are practiced by amateurs. It is the amateur, happily so named, who alone stands in a really human relation to his objects; only in amateurs do the man and his professions coincide. That is why an amateur can pour his own self into his activity, saturating it with the essence of his being; whereas things which are

SECOND NOTE

To comprehend both the intention of their specific way of looking, and to adequately comprehend the depth of information of what they have seen, we must contemplate Martin and Werner Feiersinger's photography with a certain intensity and analyze it semantically. Let's consider, for example, the vertical format of the so-called Borsalino Apartment Building (1948/52) in Alessandria [→17] designed by Ignazio Gardella.

The upper three-quarters of the format depicts the oblique view leading at a steep angle to the right, into the image's depth, of an eight-story building on an urban intersection; the lower quarter of the image is a very quiet asphalt surface. From the left and the right, the trees' mighty crowns extend into the format; in the background, on the left, more trees are discernible. The color tones cast by the solid building are, on the whole, muted, dark browns to dark reds. Shadowless, intrinsically finely shimmering, partially even enhanced with white hatching, everything is covered in a whiff of gauze. Despite a bright sky, the headlights of the cars "below" are on, reflected in the moist, lustrous street surface.

What makes the visual presence of this house so special? What do the image's other details reveal? Which associations are evoked? Which questions?

Two things catch our attention: first, the homogeneous, physical presence of the block-like massing, which, in the view across a corner, is slender. But, on account of the two continuous vertical notches—or, in other words, deep creases on the long sides—its volume seems to be arranged in a dense set-up of three or four individual towers. The differentiation of the

practiced as a profession have invariably a touch of the worst sort of lovingness, whether it takes the form of a particular one-sidedness or limitation, of subjectivity or narrowness of outlook.

G. E. KIDDER SMITH: *ITALY BUILDS*. LONDON 1955, P. 120
There is a *get up and go*, a constructive vitality in Italy which is extraordinary. Nor is this limited to building and construction alone: a few men in Milan and Turin haven shaken Detroit's automobiles to the torsion bar; the elegance from Florence and Rome is giving Paris uneasy nights; the movies from Cinécittà, in the very shadow of Rome's ancient aqueducts, are achieving a world fame rarely accorded Hollywood. The Italian novel, Italian ships, Italian sculptors and painters, the Italian motorscooter—Europe's new form of transportation—and Italian sportsmen, particularly where hair-raising velocity is concerned, are other indexes of the contagious enthusiasm and talents bursting forth from this impoverished peninsula.

prism in upright blocks and their verticality heightens—imperceptibly—the gentle stereometric undulation, causing the entire streetfront to oscillate. And all that is brought to bear as counterpoint in the second of the image's main themes: in its concentrated verticality, the dark building massing standing at slightly different angles is stopped and thwarted by the light, finely structured horizontality of the gleaming white, cantilevering roof projections, but the latter also expressively unfurl the subtle volumetric movement of the blocks, nimbly overlapping, screening, and crowning them. The verticality, on the one hand, and the lightness and movement, on the other, are evident in the narrow, uniform floor-to-ceiling windows, with a minimal floor slab as an optical and structural "break" in their linear pull, accompanied by the movable grilles of the uniform, dark-green sliding shutters.

On the left side, concealed by a tree, we sense that the pronounced hermetic massing on the corner dissolves into a white framework with balcony or loggia slabs inserted in it, that there—on the side presumably oriented to the southwest—it presents a face different from the one toward the street. Which other elements can we discern? The huge roof panels are likely stucco-coated or painted reinforced concrete structures, deliberately set apart—plastically, tectonically and chromatically—from the massing. It's plain to see that the facade has a fine-grained variegated skin—ceramic, tiles, clinker? In any case, a cladding that has to do with regional traditions, as does the shutter typology, indeed both "motifs" are heightened, becoming an unusual, abstract and seamless "union." We see a distinctly "grounded" undertone linked to the place, the city and the street, which

CARA GREENBERG: *MID-CENTURY MODERN. FURNITURE OF THE 1950s.*
NEW YORK 1984, P. 110

After several hundred years of quiescence in the furniture arts, Italy's emergence after World War II as a leader in the field came as a great surprise. From Milan, Italy's design nucleus, came furnishings with an overriding concern for style, expressed in the sculpted, curvilinear terms that had besotted the entire international design community.

But fortuitous couplings between designers and manufacturers gave Italy a creative edge. The relationships of manufacturer Cesare Cassina with Giò Ponti, Carlo de Carli, Ico Parisi, and Gianfranco Frattini exemplified the way in which Italian manufacturers were willing to risk investment in unusual designs and were able to do so because of small-scale production. Oswaldo Borsani and Tecno, Marco Zanuso and Arflex, Franco Albini and Poggi, were other fruitful alliances that resulted in the unerring execution of forward-looking designs.

is, however, accelerated artistically, transposed to a vibrant presence and urban noblesse—indeed, not a rationalist, abstract block, but a construct fine-tuned to the milieu and the building's inner workings, responding almost gesturally to them.

If we keep in mind the time of origination and the cultural mood of the postwar years in Italy, we'll detect cross-references to neorealist film and literature of this era—as well as parallels to the first postwar buildings in Denmark or in Catalonia, for example, to the comparable "blended," "vocal" urban apartment buildings by Coderch or Bohigas in Barcelona.

THIRD NOTE

My own associations with Gardella are sporadic. Early on I had encountered his tuberculosis clinic of the late thirties (also located in Alessandria), which at the time—the nineteen-seventies—seemed to me like a typical Mediterranean subversion within the framework of orthodox modernism and appeared to anticipate the aims of Ticino's *Tendenza*. In 1980, I saw his major exhibition at the first, now legendary Venice Architecture Biennale, where he—with Mario Ridolfi and Philip Johnson—was presented as one of the original "fathers" of postmodernism. But at that time in Vienna we felt closer to Gardella's "disciples"—for instance, Aldo Rossi or Vittorio Gregotti—aside from the fact that around 1970 my personal contact to the Milan scene was already primarily influenced by the rapport with the, at the time, very youngest revolutionary generation of northern Italians. This calls for a brief autobiographical excursus: for an architecture student of 1967/68, *Domus* was, of course, the most spectacular, worldly, leading

IGNAZIO GARDELLA. EXHIBITION CATALOGUE, HARVARD UNIVERSITY, GRADUATE SCHOOL OF DESIGN, BOSTON 1986, P. 15–16
The house for employees of the Borsalino factory rises on the far side of a wide, tree-lined street, where city traffic is intense, and which forms the inner boundary of the old downtown section of the city. I wanted all the apartments—which contain two or three bedrooms plus a kitchen and bathroom—to have connecting living rooms. Thus, to the north they face on the street and on the city, visually sharing in city life, while to the south they enjoy a view of the countryside and the distant Alps as well as a better exposure to the sun. This choice led to a successive widening and narrowing of the building, which could also be obtained with regular cubic volumes, of different depths, placed one beside the other but in marked relief. I preferred, instead ... to give the facades a more continuous and less violent course, by means of inclined planes on the street front, and slight reliefs on the south front.

source of information, with strong competition, of course, from London's *Architectural Design*, which more clearly heralded the revolutionary, casual and brash freshness of British pop culture than was conveyed in the always bourgeoisie-tinged, cosmopolitan elegance of *Domus*. With the work of *Missing Link* (which Angela Hareiter, Adolf Krischanitz and I formed in 1970 while still students) we moved away from the hedonist technicist exuberance of the "vanilla-cream bubbles, capsules and plug-in visions" of the groups from Vienna and London and moved farther still from concrete architecture programs or functionalist design concepts toward critical theory and their representation in artistic, performative techniques.

Particularly in Italy, in the already virulent environment of *Architettura radicale*, this tendency, as well as its cross-connections to *Arte povera*, was immediately and vividly reviewed. My direct and indirect partners in discourse from 1972 to 1976 weren't Peter Cook or Günther Feuerstein, but rather Alessandro Mendini, Adolfo Natalini, Ugo La Pietra, Andrea Branzi, Franco Raggi, Davide Mosoni, Paola Navone, and many others. When I visited Milan, it became apparent that these restless and unconventional creative minds—inspired by Pasolini, Pistoletto, and Sottsass, by Croce, Calvino and Cacciari, by Musil, Freud, and Loos—were, with respect to journalism, institutions, and commissions, much better integrated in a context both rich and close-knit, open and inquisitive, than we were in Vienna.

To take Gardella as case in point: the legacy spans generations, from the war years and the Antifascist Resistance to the present day. The nation's commerce—during fascism and the postwar boom—was patriarchically run by innovative firms that had committed themselves to resisting the

The continuity of the fronts is accentuated by the finish in dark brown terracotta tiles which covers the structure of the building with a continuous surface, a solution in contrast with a fashion then current in Italy of leaving the structural grid in view to highlight and clearly contrast the difference between "structure" and "infill."

It was considered an error, almost a deviation from rationalist orthodoxy not to do this … I also wanted the building to be an architecturally complete volume, which could not be "sliced" indifferently at any point like a sausage. At the top, the edifice finds its architectural limit in the roofing slabs which cantilever out for about six feet. They rest on beams set at regular intervals which give a modular dimension in contrast with the *mouvementé* and irregular course of the fronts … The materials and colours used are few: the brown terracotta tiles of the finish which pick up a local tradition, the white painted door and window frames, the sliding shutters painted dark green, the light grey plaster of the structural elements.

ideologization of culture and put their efforts into avant-garde aims, with all of the attendant ambivalence …

It wasn't until after 1976, when I was catching up on the critical history of modernism in the context of the social-democratic reforms of *Red Vienna* of the nineteen-twenties, that I made the parallel discovery of the every bit as rich and conflict-laden (and there, the discourse was even sharper and broader, and more profoundly commented and propagated) evolution of architecture: the modernism of Mussolini's fascism and then the counter-movements in neorealism of the postwar years and in the broad, undogmatic pluralism of the years of the economic boom.

Nota bene: Gardella hailed from a dynasty of architects dating back to the nineteenth century; one of his most important clients, related to him by marriage, was the Borsalino family, maker of the renowned hats, one of the major entrepreneurial families of the founding period in Piedmont, which even before 1938 had exported far and wide, and after 1945 further cultivated their brands worldwide, which, like the Olivetti, Fiat, Pirelli, Alfa Romeo dynasties, left marks on their locales and home cities—with all the accompanying friction—economically, socially and architecturally.

It comes as no surprise to read that as early as 1947, Gardella also established—with Luigi Caccia Dominioni and others—a design and furniture business, the firm *Azucena*, which produced modern pieces of furniture designed by architects, and continually supplied Caccia Dominioni and Gardella's projects with complete furnishings, one of the pioneering achievements in this genre in Italy next to the presently better-known examples by Cassina, Zanotta, Tecno, Artemide, Alessi, Flos, Poltronova, Pirelli, etc.

GIULIA VERONESI, IN: GERD HATJE (ED.): *ENCYCLOPAEDIA OF MODERN ARCHITECTURE*. LONDON 1963, P. 158

In and around Milan however, innumerable buildings have arisen: workers' flats, factories, houses, office blocks, churches and a number of skyscrapers (the Pirelli Building by Giò Ponti; the much discussed Torre Velasca by BBPR; the Torre Galfa by Bega; and the Torre al Parco by Magistretti). In addition to the architects of the first rational school, such as Albini, Figini, Pollini, Sartoris, Lingeri, Belgiojoso, Banfi (who died in a concentration camp), Peressutti, Rogers, Gardella, Bottoni, Mollino, Astengo, Zavanella and Nizzoli, may be named the younger generation of Zanuso, Pagani, Castiglioni, Caccia Dominioni, Latis, Fiocchi, Bernasconi, Morandi, Bassi, Viganò and Mangiarotti (known for his "glass church" at Baranzate) among others. But every city and every region is a centre where interesting architects are at work: Cocchia at Cosenza (Naples); Samonà at Minchilli (Bari); Michelucci, designer of the fine station in Florence (1936, in collaboration); the builders of the market at Pescia in Tuscany (1951); Scarpa in Venice,

FOURTH NOTE

The urban and architectural topographical inquiries of the two Feiersingers and their photographic results correspond, as it were, to an unmediated, impressionist, flâneur-like search for the enigmatic and significant moment; these are comparable to the adoring pursuit of an unattainable lover, admired from a distance and for that very reason, continuously stoking desire and fantasy; or, put differently: this study nurtures, develops and cultivates the special appeal of exploiting the subjective power of imagination encountering the "ruins" of a little-known, half-forgotten, exotic culture. These are definitely not the incidental and, in retrospect, embarrassingly disappointing vouchers of touristic scanning of the unfamiliar under the catchphrase "I was here" or "This is *my* picture of monument XYZ."

These journeys and these photos are spiritual exercises that test, open up, refresh and sharpen one's own sensitivity to what has been deliberately sought out (or, in some cases, discovered "by chance"), to interesting otherness. It is simply a matter of amplifying the poetic tension, of the aesthetic/practical repertoire of seeing and understanding space, architecture and neighborhood, of the success or failure of projects, of built and prosaic conceptions *of their time*—and not a matter of collecting ideas to be imitated. We might perhaps be able to partially comprehend their experience by positioning ourselves—unprejudiced and "naive"—in front of these photos and their precisely crafted, flat and bounded world to inquire of them as openly as possible what is obviously and also cryptically stored in them. I'll give it a try with two more images that somehow belong together.

where the best school of architecture is situated; and Albini, himself a Milanese, in Genoa, where he has built the two splendid museums of the Palazzo Bianco (1951) and San Lorenzo (1954–56).

LEONARDO BENEVOLO: *HISTORY OF MODERN ARCHITECTURE. VOLUME TWO.* CAMBRIDGE, MASSACHUSETTS 1971, PP. 711–712

(First published in Italian in 1960)

The new ruling class, composed of young men or people who had formerly been out of favour, was full of enthusiasm but could not be said to be really equipped to deal with the serious tasks awaiting it ... In the field of architecture, some of those who had waged the first battle for modern architecture, and perhaps the greatest, were dead: G. L. Banfi, R. Giolli, G. Pagano, E. Persico, G. Terragni. But at first these uncertainties were swept aside by a new, intense sensation: that of having once again made contact with reality, of seeing the things around one with new eyes, as if for the first time, and particularly

FIFTH NOTE

The vertical format [→49] shows a typical frayed situation on the edge of a large city, a standard nine-story rental apartment building of recent vintage next to lower, suburban buildings, industrial and commercial facilities, vacant and unkempt parcels of land following a demolition; fragmentary sidewalks, fences with slapdash posters, graffiti. Though it is daytime, not much urban life is visible. The image is composed such that the horizon bisects the vertical format; the street depicted runs steeply back to the left with its vanishing point just beyond the image's left-hand edge, while the frontage lines perpendicular to this street are nearly parallel to the image's frame, and therefore have a vanishing point "at infinity."

This image's perspectival dramaturgy definitely has to do with (deliberate) essential features of the peripheral, of the sub-urban. If we divide the format into six fields equal in size, the one to the right of the center straddles the horizon and is filled with a rather enigmatic, erratic part of the building that appears to continue beyond the edge of the image and which, due to a recent demolition along its fire wall, is revealed with respect to both time and space—and, as the rubble chute hanging out the upper window suggests, even subjected to cryptic interventions.

What is irritating about the photo—the situation depicted—is the upper part of the building. Like the head of a moray eel or the stern of a ship it extends past a dull, ducked-down base into the street. Upon closer inspection of this conspicuous physiognomy we'll recognize all sorts of conflicting, even surreal aspects: the cantilever—estimated at more than five meters—is supported by gently curved, elegantly tapering reinforced

those closest to one, hitherto masked by patriotic rhetoric or veiled with platitudes. It was this sensation that gave rise to so-called "neo-realism" which found its best means of expression in the cinema, but influenced Italian culture in general in a variety of ways. The films of Rossellini and De Sica, the theatre of Eduardo, the paintings of Guttuso, the architecture of Ridolfi at Terni and the Tiburtino district in Rome have in common the desire to keep close to everyday reality, concrete and solid …

TELEFONIA
WIND
vodafone

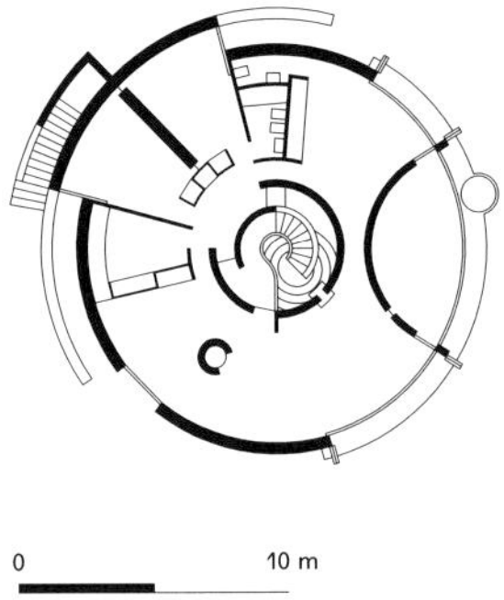

1954–55

MARCELLO D'OLIVO

HOLIDAY HOME

LIGNANO PINETA, RAGGIO DI LEVANTE, ARCO DEL MAESTRALE

The resort town of Lignano Pineta granted D'Olivo a number of opportunities to experiment with circular forms. Beginning in 1952, he developed a spiral-shaped land-use plan for the town center. His work on a serpentine mixed-use building named *Il Treno* began the same year and lasted until 1960. He also designed two adjacent circular residences at the seafront. Both of them have covered outdoor spaces at street level, living spaces on the upper level and roof terraces, but otherwise the designs take diverging paths. The one in the east (1955–1957) has several loosely distributed, curved walls. The one documented here, in contrast, seems contained and introverted, but has a surprising space: at its center it is hollowed out and open to the sky, and a curved stair within it leads up to the entrance.

1954–60

MARIO BACCIOCCHI

AGIP GAS STATION
MILAN, PIAZZALE ACCURSIO

In the postwar era, Mario Bacciocchi was Italy's gas station architect par excellence. The standardized station types he developed for Agip have a strong identity. They are freestanding structures located both in cityscapes and landscapes throughout Italy. The station depicted here, however, is one of a kind. Bacciocchi devised it expressly for this tapering corner site. In this design his trademark detail is absent: the striking projecting roof folded down on one edge. Instead he enlisted an extremely thin projecting roof and a dynamic yet supple formal vocabulary reminiscent of early drawings by Erich Mendelsohn. The effect of the roof's considerable cantilever is reinforced by the dissolution of the corner. Emphasis is placed on two fundamental themes: speed and dynamics.

stazione Musocco
sacco

1954–68

MARIO RIDOLFI, WOLFGANG FRANKL

OLIVETTI PRESCHOOL

IVREA, CANTON VESCO, VIALE DELLA LIBERAZIONE 4

This preschool erected for the children of Olivetti employees is considered one of Ridolfi & Frankl's finest designs. But it is also a paragon of Italian neorealist architecture. Situated amid modest rows of workers' housing, the preschool is distinguished by its picturesque conception, fine craftsmanship and the use of traditional materials such as wood and stone. The two-story office wing lines the street [→**66**]; the low-slung classroom pavilions extend across the site, connected by a covered passage and several covered terraces. The roofs are accessible as well, and are inhabited by cube-like structures with brick grilles. Metal structures reminiscent of garden trellises also crown the preschool. Below them skylights dot the roofs.

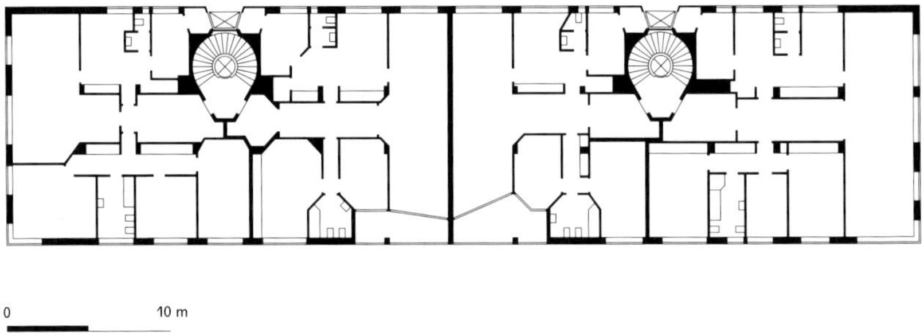

1955–57

LUIGI CACCIA DOMINIONI

APARTMENT BUILDING
MILAN, VIA IPPOLITO NIEVO 28/1

This high-rise is part of a residential development in which the buildings are sited parallel to one another. Although the height and depth of the structures were predetermined, Caccia Dominioni's stands out from the pack. His selection of a reinforced concrete frame structure gave him the freedom to design the floor plans as he saw fit. It also facilitated a playful approach to the design of the building envelope: the arrangement of the windows reflects the nuances of the various floor plans. This yields a depictive composition made up of different window formats. Caccia Dominioni built another similar apartment house along the same stretch (Via Ippolito Nievo 10). Its facade is clad in reddish brown ceramic tiles [→**71**].

BN 967DC

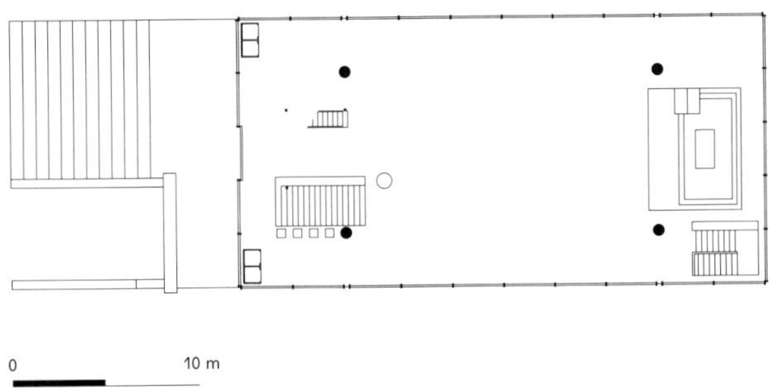

1956–57

ANGELO MANGIAROTTI, BRUNO MORASSUTTI

CHIESA MATER MISERICORDIAE

MILAN, BARANZATE, VIA DELLA CONCILIAZIONE 22–24

In a rectangular courtyard, shielded from its surroundings by a perimeter wall, stands the Glass Church. The courtyard serves as a buffer and defines a sacred realm. The architects placed a plinth of the same height as the wall in it and put an abstract glazed structure on top of the plinth. The crystalline object's structure can only be experienced inside the building: it consists of four round concrete columns that support a ceiling of prefabricated concrete units. The entrance sequence passes through a symbolic threshold: a ramp leads down to the forecourt of the baptismal chapel. From the chapel, a stairway leads up to the center of the church. To attend mass, worshippers enter the space directly from the outdoors through a sliding glass door. A layer of polystyrene between the panes of the double glazing diffuses the light entering the sanctuary.

COSI COME TE

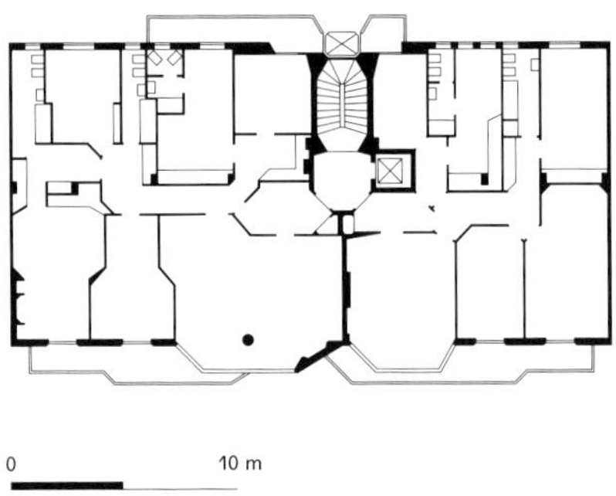

1956–59

LUIGI CACCIA DOMINIONI

APARTMENT BUILDING
MILAN, VIA GIUSEPPE VIGONI 13

The apartment building fills a gap in the urban fabric. The compact structure, with two units per floor, was designed with the interiors in mind: without taking the exterior appearance into account, Caccia Dominioni considered ideal room sizes and sequences, and how daylight would enter the spaces. On the one hand, the living rooms have extensively glazed bay windows; on the other, the bedrooms have French doors with shutters typical of the region. This makes the different functions legible in the facade. Caccia Dominioni used balconies to tie them together. The seemingly decorative ribbons in the notch between the two bay windows are in fact chimneys.

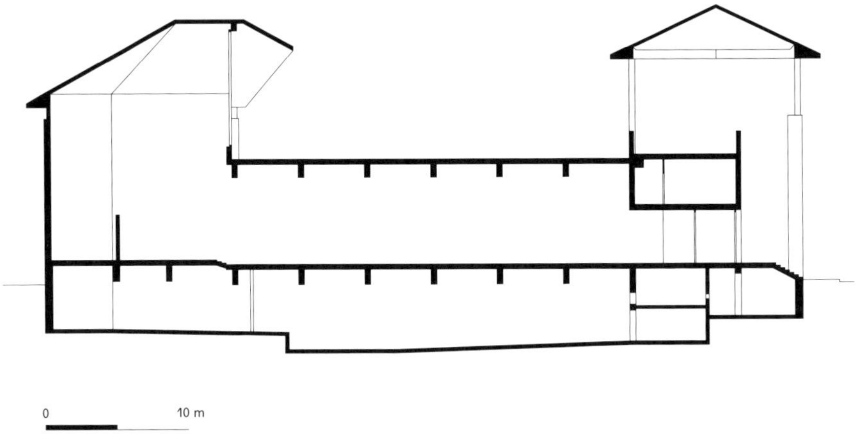

1956–60

PIER GIACOMO CASTIGLIONI, ACHILLE CASTIGLIONI

CHIESA SAN GABRIELE ARCANGELO IN MATER DEI
MILAN, VIA TERMOPILI

This church is one of the few works of architecture by the industrial designers Pier Giacomo and Achille Castiglioni. Fronting the street are the parsonage and a large loggia. The church itself is set back from the street, situated perpendicular to it and bordered by a courtyard. A certain affinity to Caccia Dominioni is evident in the facade. Indeed, following their studies, Livio, the eldest of the Castiglioni brothers, and Pier Giacomo had worked with Caccia Dominioni. The nave of the church is plastered and painted brick red; all other wall surfaces are clad in a brick veneer. The Y-shaped columns and the loggia's roof structure are in reinforced concrete. The interior is strikingly simple. A large multi-purpose space is situated below the church.

CB 067BP

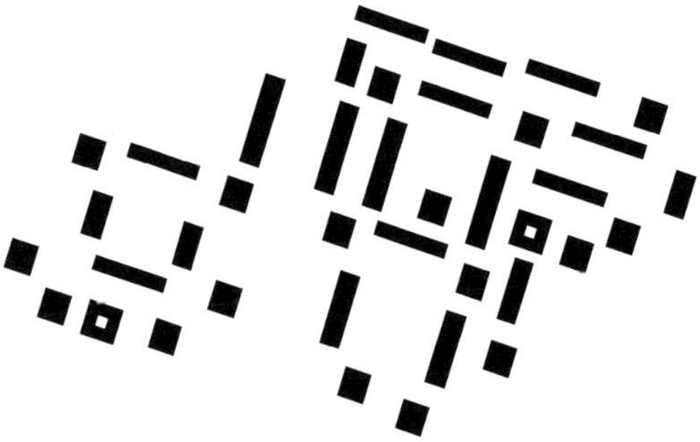

M 1:5000

1956–63

MARIO RIDOLFI, WOLFGANG FRANKL

VILLAGGIO COORDINATO

TREVISO, VIA SICILIA, VIA CALABRIA, LARGO TRE VENEZIE

Prior to the Second World War, Ridolfi & Frankl were adherents of *Razionalismo*. After the war, they became important representatives of *Neorealismo*. Like their most renowned buildings—the Quartiere Tiburtino (1949–55) and the residential high-rises on Via Etiopia (1949–56), both in Rome—the project in Treviso is marked by a return to simple construction methods, as well as by craftsmanship, regional techniques, and, above all, picturesque design. Some of the piazzas could almost be mistaken for the backdrops for a neorealist film. The complex, situated on the edge of Treviso, is made up of a series of row houses, low-slung apartment buildings, courtyard buildings, and seventeen similar towers. The variation in the towers occurs in the crenellation.

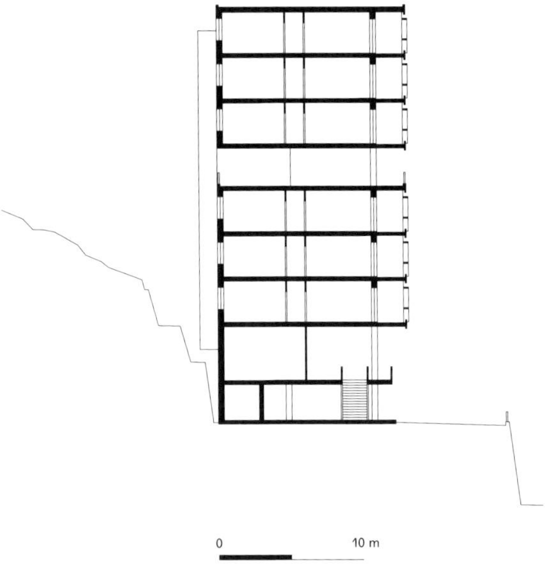

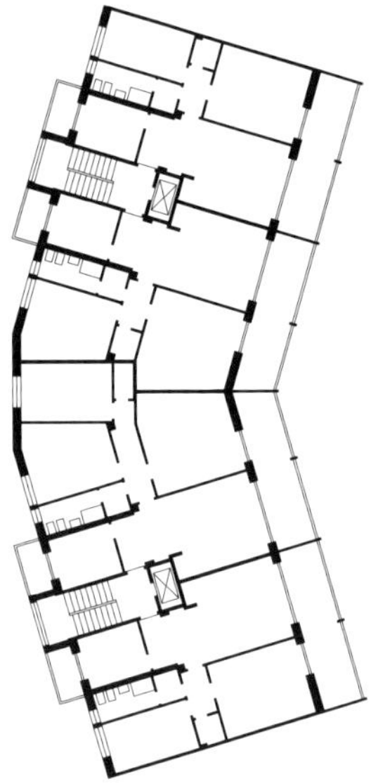

1956–68

LUIGI CARLO DANERI

FORTE QUEZZI HOUSING COMPLEX
GENOA, VIA LORIA, VIA FEA, VIA MODIGLIONI

INA-Casa, the federal housing agency, commissioned this gigantic complex. High above Genoa and with a view of the sea, five serpentine apartment blocks follow the contours of the hillside. Consequently, the complex has been dubbed *Il Biscione* (the large snake). A total of thirty-five architects were involved in the planning. A group led by Robaldo Morozzo della Rocca was responsible for the lowermost snake [→**92**]. A second group, headed by Angelo Sibilla, was in charge of the structure with a four-story base and a two-story crown [→**93**]. Daneri designed the part situated farthest up the slope as a string of apartments; the structure has thirty-four staircases—each providing access to two apartments per floor—and a series of identical loggias; he organized the building massing in two blocks with three levels each, separated by an open promenade level.

N M 1:5000

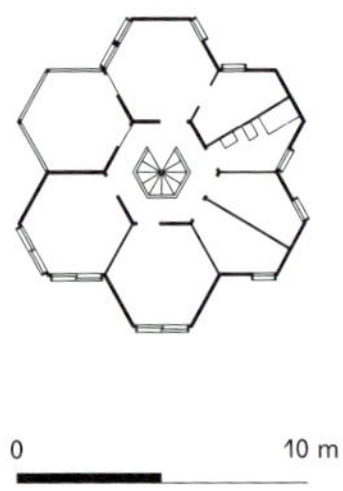

VITTORIO GIORGINI
HEXAGON
BARATTI

The Hexagon in Baratti was Giorgini's first building—his own summer house on a plateau above the Mediterranean. The aim was to develop a modular building system. Structurally the house consists of six connected, one-legged "tables." Each leg—or pylon—rests on a sphere embedded in a hexagonal concrete foundation. Room units were positioned atop the tables. Giorgini placed a hexagonal spiral staircase at the center of the structure. The stair leads from below the house to a trap door—bringing to mind a tree house. Slender steel rods were inserted—as retrofitting—between the pylons to provide additional stiffness to the house.

1957

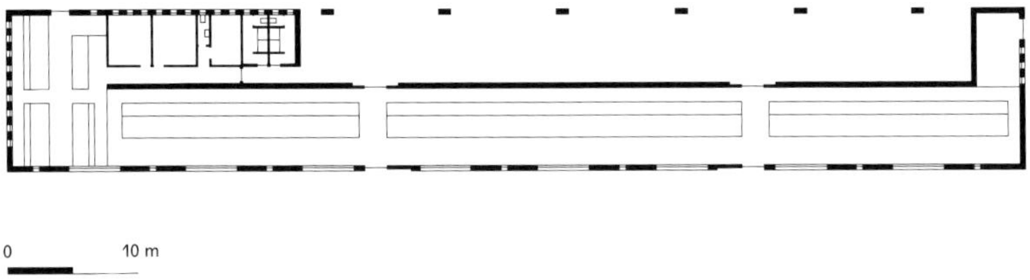

1957–58

GIORGIO RAINERI

OLIVETTI FARM
MONTALENGHE, VIA ROMA

Raineri designed this project for *I-RUR*, an agrarian cooperative set up by Adriano Olivetti in an effort to modernize the agriculture of the Canavese region. The barn is divided in two parts. The south-facing half contains the cow stalls. The north-facing half, the taller of the two, contains a hay barn. The ventilation elements for both parts are integrated in the central wall; these include a series of ventilation chimneys for the cow stalls and brick latticework to cross-ventilate the stored hay.

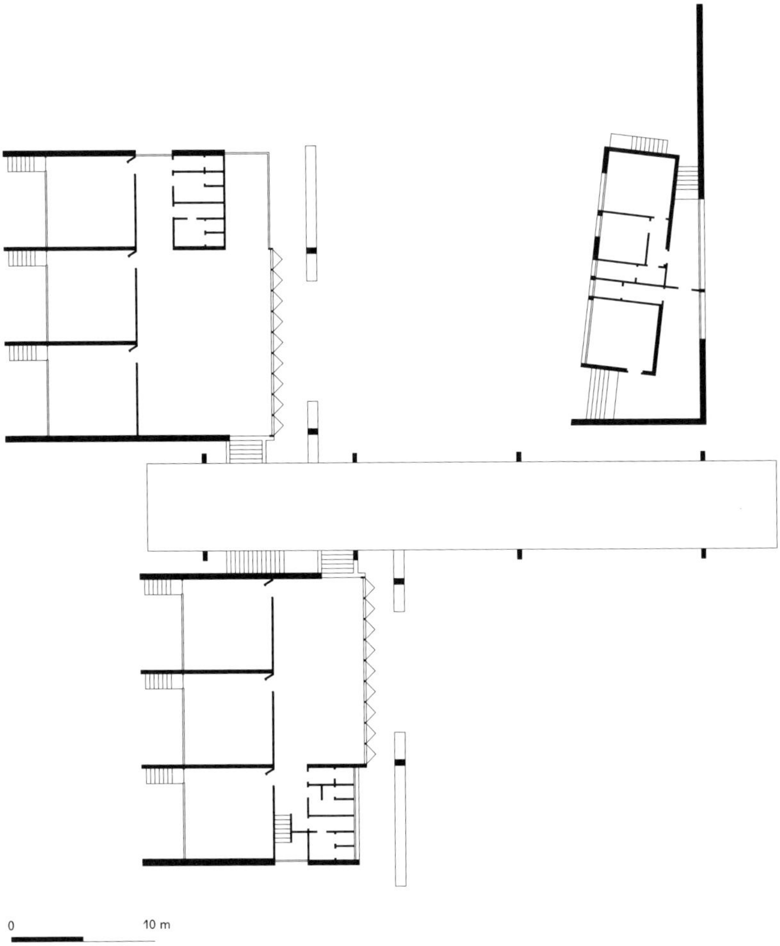

1957–58

ENRICO CASTIGLIONI

SCHOOL

BUSTO ARSIZIO, VIA MINGHETTI 20, VIALE STELVIO

This school is made up to two freestanding pavilions with a total of six classrooms, a compact administration building with an apartment for the custodian, and a passageway sheltered by a swooping roof that links the different buildings. Here Castiglioni employs the structural members as ornament and celebrates the transferal of loads: a honeycomb-shaped grille directs the ceiling-beam forces into the struts and, at the same time, reflects sunlight. The glazed facade behind it was originally zigzagged: the single panes of glass were framed in slender steel profiles. The present skin is flat and double-glazed, but the former version is still legible in the vestiges of the original steel profiles.

concrete beams; the part of the building below is cut off obliquely toward the street, sheathed in old roof tiles, and, on its facade, has a large ornamental, grille-like screened opening, tending toward the enigmatic.

The "head," situated at the height of the second floor, has, as mentioned, a modern, not exactly low-brow, load-bearing structure, and, in contrast, a conventional pitched roof, banally clad in corrugated fiber-cement sheets; the long side is very transparent—it is glazed along the entire length in a modular frame system (steel?) that also extends into the roof contour and perhaps corresponds with the positions of the rafters; in any case, it indicates a structure of the industrial sort, so generously laid out that it can't possibly come to a close in ten meters, that it in fact suggests a series, a continuation. And on its short end this light, modern, though not modernist-seeming, structure with a cyclopic, banal eye looks at the city, somewhere into the vastness of the area.

In the otherwise trivial context exists a presumably small "drama"—and this continues to develop and decipher itself, if we go around the corner, made possible for us by a second photo taken as a "counter-shot." And here the whole building behind the absurd headpiece is revealed: thin-as-a-rake barracks, some one hundred meters long, woven entirely of steel and glass. It overlaps and spans an impenetrable piecemeal base, whose irregular contours and openings are held together visually by a skin of rust-toned hexagonal tiles—a skin that at some locations is perforated, veil-like, by a ceramic grille of the same format as the tiles.

We encounter a formal complex phenomenology that brings to mind the "analogous" architecture that was propagated around 1980 in German-

ULRICH GREGOR, ENNO PATALAS: *GESCHICHTE DES FILMS. VOLUME 2.* 1940–1960. REINBECK BEI HAMBURG 1976, PP. 273–274

After 1945, in Italy the art of moviemaking became the avant-garde of all the European countries that had endured the war ... Rosselini's first postwar movies—*Roma città aperta* (1945) and *Paisà* (1945)—represent neorealism in its "purest" form, in which seemingly only the reality of the occurrences on the screen does the directing ... The tragic episodes of the movies are so convincing not only because they occur, as it were, "in the margins" of the action, brought about by the dramaturgy, but also because Rosselini keeps them in balance with comical and grotesque scenes.

speaking Switzerland, and which at the time took the rough, "dirty realism" of industrial districts or railway yards as role model as well as for multi-layered use of vacant, anonymous urban districts and their hybrid building typologies. Elevated to academia and filtered, this sensibility lives on in different facets of contemporary architecture, in German-Swiss cantons—and in all, taking a turn toward more sleekness and commitment, the melancholic-critical poesy and marginal sensibility of Aldo Rossi still resonates ...

But built here, on the south side of Milan, as it turns out, in 1956! Architect Luigi Caccia Dominioni? Never heard of him? He takes up considerable space in the Feiersingers' album—a veritable "discovery," a distinct, difficult-to-grasp cosmos in *Pianeta Milano*! We'll come back to it later. For this corner on Via Filippo Brunelleschi (!) it may suffice to mention that it was a matter of linking and transforming two existing office wings of a large mechanical-engineering firm and extending and covering them with a light, endless-seeming hull.

SIXTH NOTE

Earlier I mentioned a photo [→44] that should be seen in the context of the building under discussion. It shows a world-renowned modern symbol of Milan, Torre Velasca, in the center of the city, only five hundred meters from the cathedral, completed in 1957, at the same time as the previous building, designed by Studio BBPR (Lodovico Belgiojoso, Enrico Peressutti, Ernesto Nathan Rogers). In the late nineteen-fifties this project was the focus of international architectural debate and marked a turning point that

ANDRÉ BAZIN: *LADRI DI BICICLETTE*, IN: ROBERT FISCHER (ED.): WAS IST FILM? BERLIN 2004; REPRINTED IN: FAHRRADDIEBE. EIN FILM VON VITTORIO DE SICA. ALAMODE FILM. MUNICH 2008, DVD PAMPHLET, PP. 6 AND 18

Ladri di biciclette fulfils all the neorealist principles that one can derive from the best Italian movies since 1946. The "popular," even populist, plot: an episode in the day-to-day life of a common worker. And by no means one of the extraordinary events of the sort that happen à la Gabin to the preordained workers. No crime of passion, no stupendous transgression. In other words, nothing that simply shifts the tragedies once reserved for the Greek Gods into the exotic proletarian milieu. Instead, an insignificant, even banal, occurrence: a worker spends the entire day in Rome looking in vain for the bicycle someone has stolen from him ... The plot did not exist in advance as an essence, but follows from the existence of what has already been narrated: that is the "integral" of reality. De Sica's greatest achievement—others have not even come close to it—is that he has succeeded in developing a filmic dialectic that is able to overcome the

also emphatically explains the Italian situation of this era. The composition of the photo—one that they selected and that I have here in front of me—is again very illuminating.

The skyscraper is moved right in the vertical axis of the cropped image, showing a slightly oblique view—the shorter front facing us and in the shade, the longer one brightened by low-altitude sunlight—and that is certainly afternoon light, a low west-southwest sun, so we are definitely looking at the tower from the north. The nine- and ten-story buildings in front, erected during the same time period, convey the stoic grandeur of the day-to-day reconstruction work of the northern Italian metropoles.

With its twenty-seven stories and at a height of one hundred meters, *Torre Velasca* stays (as required) slightly below the cathedral's apex (Vienna's *Ringturm* [Ring Tower] by Erich Boltenstern—construction began later and was completed earlier—is seventy-three meters tall and one kilometer away from St. Stephen's Cathedral).

The photo presents the tower's striking silhouette, the slender shaft, the "head" cantilevering on all sides, and the structural verticals that organize the fronts and evenly surround the tower and support the upper part obliquely with scaffolding-like struts.

At the time, this form was spontaneously critiqued as a modern transformation of the character of medieval Italian towers, as a memento of tower houses and turrets celebrated but also strongly criticized by the architectural elite. In 1959, at the 11th CIAM Congress in Otterlo, the debate centered on this building and turned out to be a catalyst to the drifting apart of positions within the architectural avant-garde, which then gave

contradiction between theatrical plot and mere occurrence. From this perspective, *Ladri di biciclette* is one of the first examples of pure cinema. No more actors, no story, no mise-en-scène. Ultimately, in the consummate aesthetic illusion of reality, that means: no more cinema.

BENEVOLO, OP. CIT., PP. 720–722
In the Torre Velasca in Milan (completed in 1958) the studio B.B.P.R. carried off the singular attempt at treating the facade of a skyscraper as a formally finite episode, while this type of building was always interpreted as a rhythmic structure, open and potentially extensible. The elevation of the tower is divided into two perfectly inter-balanced parts, while the vertical supporting elements, protruding from the base to the summit, serve to mediate between the general bulk of the building and the uniform openings of the single floors—as in Sullivan—by replacing the uniform rhythm with a continuous gradation and by a particularly careful modulation of the detachment of the projection.

up once and for all on the vision to formulate a globally valid planning methodology—it was CIAM's final act.

The publication of the discussions between Peter Smithson, Jacob Berend Bakema, on the one hand, and Ernesto Nathan Rogers, Giancarlo de Carlo, on the other, are still readable, ravishing documents of this search for a consensus on how to deal with the—in the meantime, meaningless—dogmas of the heroic phase of modernism.

I had seen the building in photos (though I hadn't encountered it while at the university) and didn't see it in situ until 1975, and even then, didn't engage with it very much. But while tracking down the sources over the last few days, the full complexity of the design, its larger context, and its position at the crossroads of European postwar architecture emerges. Some of this explosive power can, to be sure, be recognized and comprehended by carefully reading the photos.

SEVENTH NOTE

The photo shows Torre Velasca in light conditions that make the details of the building form's plasticity clearly legible. If you look very closely, the changes in rhythm become discernible: the differences between the head and the shaft, and the differentiated treatment of the corners. The tectonics of the tower suggest "strong skin" and "structure on the outside," tending toward heterotrophic—an antithesis to the tenets of the Mies van der Rohe School (autonomous structure, envelope separate from structure, dematerialized as curtain, tending toward isotropic …). The vertical main lines of thrust change in rhythm from the bottom to the top; the distribution of the

In this way there is a mainly contemplative relationship between the building and its urban setting. According to Rogers, the tower aims, without actually following the style of any of its buildings, "culturally to summarize the atmosphere of the city of Milan, its elusive yet pervasive mood"; its singularity and uniqueness derive precisely from the fact that it appears as an isolated contrast, a summary of the preexisting landscape; it would be impossible to see in it even the faintest allusion to any building type which could be multiplied to change that same landscape … The difficulty of tackling, above a certain scale, the problems which were ever more rapidly conditioning the life of the modern city, and therefore the failure in continuity between architectural and town-planning involvement. This is the crucial point in present day Italian architectural thought, and it is only by considering all other facts within this framework—including the excellent production of the best architects—that one can assess their significance.

apertures is slightly irregular. The openings in the upper part contrast with the ones below, suggesting a different function. Moreover, at the top, the left and right corners differ from one another and are dissolved asymmetrically. If you look very closely, you will notice that the shaft's edges are chamfered and penetrated by narrow, diagonal window apertures; between shaft and head is a shaded caesura, a visual-volumetric break or joint, presumably an intermediate service level.

The building envelope, which rises up continuously as "heavy armor," shows itself to be finely modulated—which also implies that the variety carries over to the interiors, to the floor plans. As the position of the sun in the photo suggests, the tower does not stand in the north–south axis. Rather, this passes diagonally through the floor plan—the visible narrow side, which presently faces away from the sun, will also receive morning sun. Thus, all four fronts receive direct sunlight over the course of the day—and this rotation is finely accentuated in the floor plan and in the plasticity ... Ernesto Nathan Rogers's explanation of the design at CIAM XI in Otterlo covers all of the relevant background information: the arrangement of the building in apartments at the top (larger floor areas, better views, roof terraces) and offices below; as well as the decisions regarding structure, material and form. Peter Smithson's replies are still noteworthy, but from a present-day standpoint, Bakema's complaint, that the building doesn't allow you to sense the autos entering the large underground garage, is odd.

Torre Velasca is not a universal formal model. It is a rationally and architecturally conceived, deliberate outcome employing the most modern means of the day, a contemporary, unique, highly contextual—and therefore

ERNESTO ROGERS, IN: JÜRGEN JOEDIKE (ED.): *DOCUMENTS OF MODERN ARCHITECTURE. CIAM '59 IN OTTERLO*. STUTTGART 1961, PP. 92–93
The building by-laws in Milan do not allow any building to be higher than the Madellina, which is at the top of the Duomo—about one hundred and six metres high. Our building is approximately one hundred metres high and within that height limitation. The general shape of the building is the result of a very rational design approach. We were required to design a building which was to be occupied partially by offices and partially by dwellings. Our studies of the space distribution requirements for the offices and dwellings led us to conclude that more space was obviously required by the dwellings per floor than by the offices. We therefore increased the floor area of the apartments and expressed this in the facade ... There are two floors underground devoted to a garage for four hundred cars; the first eighteen floors above the ground are for offices (four of these eighteen being provided with shower facilities, kitchenettes and other amenities); the eighteenth floor is a service-floor containing the machinery for the pumps and

still ambivalent, and, for that reason, still relevant result. The references attributed to it subsequently were all limited to the late Middle Ages, feudal allusions. But I detect references to modern industrial buildings, water towers, signal towers, to Iwan Leonidow's skyscraper project *Narkomtiazhprom* for Moscow's Red Square (1934) and the like.

In conclusion, back to the photo: commanding the foreground are not elegant Lancia sedans, but rather a semi-trailer loaded with construction materials, large fire doors in metal frames and—farther back—closely stacked metal frames (glazing panels?) or metallic scaffolding tubing. Those familiar with the story know that in 1950, BBPR conceived of the tower in steel and glass and then, for budgetary and technical reasons, had to laboriously redesign it in concrete and cast stone. This may ascribe a further layer of meaning to the photo's certainly not incidental, more likely purposely "anticipated," foreground.

EIGHTH NOTE, AFTERTHOUGHT TO SEVENTH NOTE

Other photos [→31, 32, 33] show a mixed-use complex that was built only two blocks away at the same time as Torre Velasca. In the images the situation seems, like before, metropolitan and dramatically dense, conflict-laden. A white, sharp-edged and rigorous modernist architecture forges ahead in the tight urban space. Indeed, it is obvious that this was not a matter of stubbornly carrying out a universalist design with "pure" geometry or typology.

Most striking is the—let's say—elegant/brutal gesture, in which a gigantic, menacing bow of a ship pushes forward to the street "from the

other things the people in the building require; the next eight floors are devoted to apartments, the last two of which are penthouses with roof garden facilities ... The structure of the building is concrete, although our original conception of it was in steel. The building was studied for many years and underwent many changes, but our general conception of the space distribution remained the same. The construction system ... was changed because the structure in steel in Italy would have been too expensive: thirty percent more expensive. The panels between the columns are prefabricated elements. They are within the limits of our economy and our building technology in Italy. We have used windows of more or less standard production ... We decided to devise a flexible system which would allow the interchanging of the voids and the panels in the facade ... If this building by chance of circumstances has taken the shape that reminds you of the past, that is not the main point of the problem.

depths of the space" and with full force mounts a low row of shops lining the street. At the center this glazed base, presumably with offices on the upper level, bridges the driveway into a narrow courtyard, behind which even taller (I count thirteen stories) apartment blocks loom, and on the photo's left edge the plinth rises again obliquely upward, partially adding an additional story—and it almost creates the impression that the dashing bow of a ship has run aground on this low jetty and with its weight has indented the plinth slightly, but managed to come to a stop just in the nick of time.

It is likely the case that this is an attempt to keep the monumentally dimensioned, sharp-edged front from crashing unmediated onto the sidewalk and, to introduce a mediating scale between the tall buildings and the narrow street. On the far left of the image, we recognize that the street continues back at an unusual angle, and thus the evidence is mounting that here a quite high density was "made to measure," taking into account the specific routes of streets and the trajectories within this new fabric with regards to lighting, daylighting, minimum setbacks, etc., and that the pure geometries of the unequivocally modernist approach are distorted into several irregular creases, slants, and heights. Next we take a look at the date and the architect: from 1949 to 1956, Luigi Moretti (who, as a versatile wanderer between ideologies, made his mark with his first buildings for Mussolini). A search via Google Maps for the a aerial view of this corner on Corso Italia once and for all solves the riddle of the complex configuration. The project shows a formal outcome of modernism that is undogmatic, contextual, entirely site-specific, and inimitably resilient.

PETER SMITHSON, IN: JOEDICKE, OP. CIT., PP. 94–95
Now I suggest that you, in a way, created a model here which has included certain consequences which, if you had been aware of your position in society and your position in the development of things, you would have seen are dangerous. Such a development contains the possibility of other people's doing similar things in a worse way. The strength of Le Corbusier and Mies van der Rohe lies in the fact that their written work—their thoughts—and their buildings are one. To me they are in themselves a model. By that I mean they are pedagogic too: an answer to the problem as it is, and they have the generalizing aspect of all problems of such a nature in such a time. For me there is a certain element of irresponsibility in this building.

NINTH NOTE

Feiersinger's collection of photos reveals blind spots in a genre in which it was believed that all the bases had been covered. In terms of composition, the images do not indulge in the formal autism of professional architectural photography, nor in the situational *auteur* photography dedicated to everyday matters. The building depicted stands, of course, at the center of attention, yet is usually "orchestrated" in such fashion that the peripheral or contextual qualities—unrelated to the building per se—can also play a part. Inasmuch, this way of seeing unobtrusively and discreetly opens up the depicted spaces again to aspects that had become overgrown and appropriated. It's usually little things: the decision where to place the camera, how the subject is framed in the finder, the way a "chance" foreground is incorporated or the mood of the light is controlled. Aside from that, the collection as a whole offers a panorama-like, almost mannerist field study that brings together stylistic opposites in a relaxed manner and supplies the isolated subject with a sounding board of diverging contexts. In this way the seemingly complete, everything's-been-checked-off-the-list perspective can be opened up again and give them (the authors of the images) and us (the observers) refreshing, instructive visual and cerebral experiences.

The following three images, or as the case may be, subjects, provide a nice cross-section of this sort: all three buildings originated around 1958, all are structurally imposing, with concrete as the primary building material—and what a contrast in the results and positions. And, at the same time: what a concordance in the accentuation, giving full rein to the respective imagination.

E. ROGERS, IN: JOEDICKE, OP. CIT., P. 96

I think that the only architect of the present who has had this same effect (= Palladio) is Mies van der Rohe. For he is the only architect who is really modern in the sense that Palladio was in his time. He who copies Le Corbusier or Gropius is an imbecile. For all their products are absolutely personal. You cannot learn form from Le Corbusier or from Gropius. There is much to be learnt from these people but you cannot learn the lesson of form. I think that the fundamentals of modern architecture came from Gropius, he taught us the methods but not the models in the sense of forms.

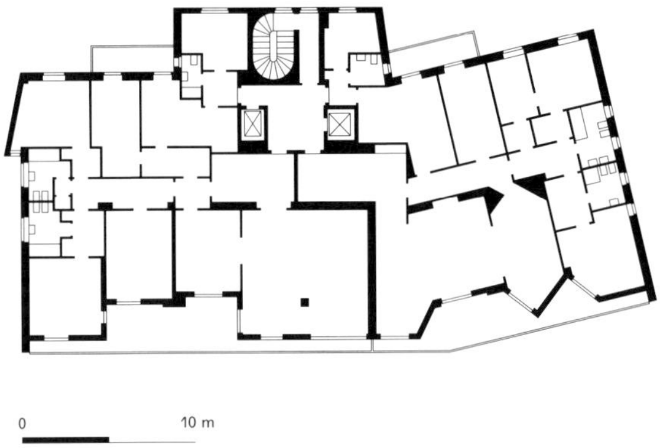

GIULIO MINOLETTI

APARTMENT BUILDING

MILAN, CORSO DI PORTA ROMANA 76/2

1957–59

Giardino d'Arcadia, a lush hidden garden in the heart of Milan, is the setting for this remarkable apartment building. With Minoletti's arrangement of fourteen large apartments side by side and on top of each other, he offered a new take on the *villa multipla*—stacked villas. The units all have a main entrance and a staff entrance. The balcony is the datum line. Behind it, every floor plan is unique. There are two other versions of the *villa multipla* in the immediate vicinity: the neighboring apartment building, an Ignazio Gardella project (1951–53) and, at the other end of the park, the Casa della Meridiana (1925) by Giuseppe de Finetti, who had studied under Adolf Loos. Finetti's design was one of the first to employ this concept.

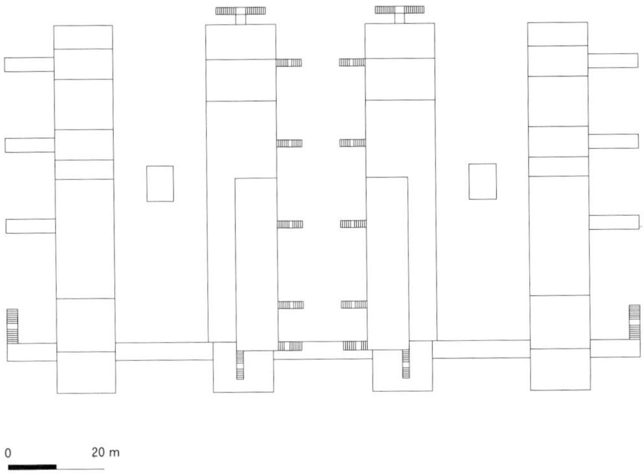

1957–59

LEONARDO SAVIOLI

VILLAGGIO BELVEDERE HOUSING COMPLEX
PISTOIA, PIAZZA BELVEDERE, VIA DEI TIGLI

INA-Casa, the federal housing agency, set out to improve the architectural design of subsidized dwellings: this complex is a good example of these efforts. Savioli drew up a structure consisting of a framework of slender columns painted light gray and infilled with fields of yellow stucco. The various roof projections—some with considerable cantilevers—are a hallmark of Savioli's work. Special attention was devoted to the circulation within the complex and to the transitions between publicly accessible and private zones.

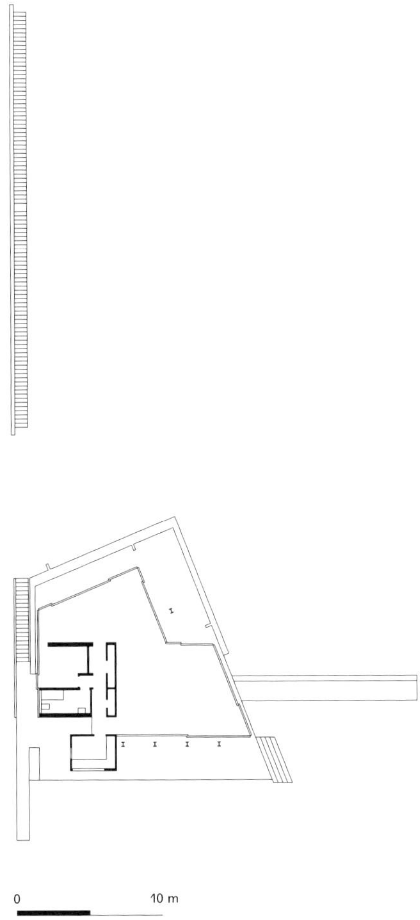

VITTORIANO VIGANÒ
HOLIDAY HOME
PORTESE, VIA BENACO

1957–60

Viganò designed this house for another architect—for André Bloc, who was also a sculptor and the founder of a variety of magazines, first and foremost *L'architecture d'aujourd'hui*. A renowned practitioner of Italian brutalism, Viganò recognized the opportunity to create a building of incomparable rawness and vigor. His abstract conception for a park-like site on Lake Garda projected a pavilion with a floor slab hovering above the terrain, a massive roof slab, slender steel columns, and sliding-glass doors. The house is positioned right at the edge of a steep slope, and roughly half of it cantilevers beyond the edge. A stair supported by a forty-meter-long concrete beam leads down to the lake. It is one of the design's most striking features—and the reason the residence is often referred to as La Scala.

N M 1:5000

1957–64

LUIGI CACCIA DOMINIONI

MIXED-USE BUILDING
MILAN, CORSO ITALIA 22–24

A number of the elements in Caccia Dominioni's repertoire are brought together in this multi-faceted project, a contextual insertion on the major thoroughfare Corso Italia: the attention to the detailing of the extravagant glass veranda, the mise-en-scène of the outdoor spaces and the skillful bracketing of the site. The polygonal tower with tiled courtyard facade revisits the *villa multipla* theme [→**106**]. There is just one apartment per story, but the floor plans vary from level to level. Residents enter the respective units directly from the elevator—the stairway serves as an escape route and contains the entrances for the personnel.

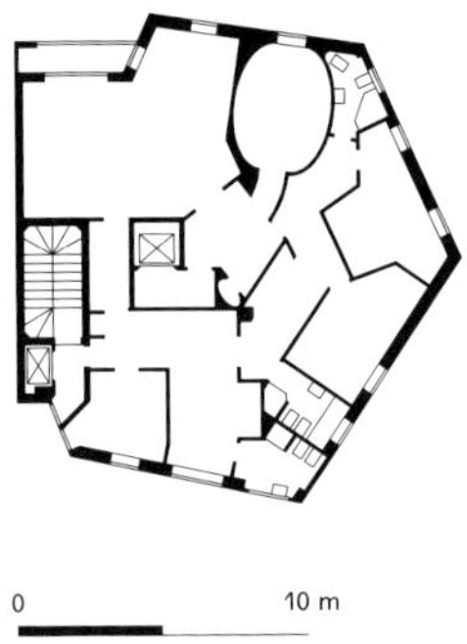

0
10 m

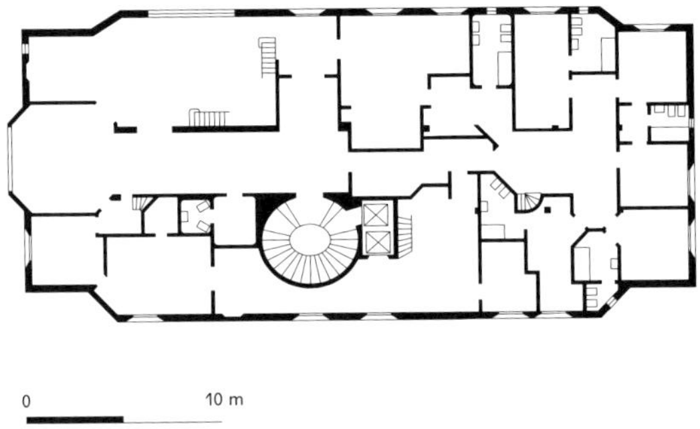

1958–64

LUIGI CACCIA DOMINIONI

RESIDENCE

MILAN, VIA PIETRO TAMBURINI 5, VIA 20 SETTEMBRE

In Italy, a freestanding urban villa is known as a *palazzetto unifamiliare*. This site is in a smart neighborhood near Parco Sempione. At first glance, Caccia Dominioni's solution to the rare design problem does not seem out of the ordinary, but this home is the epitome of understatement. Upon closer inspection, the great care the architect devoted to the detailing—for example, the oblique reveals, the curved transition of the wall to the projecting roof, and the inlaid rain pipes—can be discerned. The true extravagance, however, is contained within the building. To paraphrase Caccia Dominioni, the variety in the sequences of rooms, stairs, elevators, and corridors creates "paths and squares" that make the dwelling seem like a "small city unto itself."

VIA
TAMBURINI
0-24

1958–65

IGNAZIO GARDELLA

HOLIDAY FLATS

PINETA DI ARENZANO, VIA DELLA ROTONDA

Pineta di Arenzano is an extensive holiday community on the Ligurian coast west of Genoa. In 1956, Gardella and Marco Zanuso began work on a master plan to make this site amenable to development. They also planned a hotel named Punta San Martino (1958). By the end of the decade the community was booming and additional buildings designed by Gardella were erected. Other important Milanese firms were also engaged here. When Gardella's structure first comes into view, it appears to be just a low building with a roof garden; from this same street, situated above the flats, the sea is visible beyond the roof. At the center of the building, however, a spectacular space opens up holding a stair leading down the steep slope towards the sea. From this vantage point it becomes clear that the complex contains a significant number of residential units.

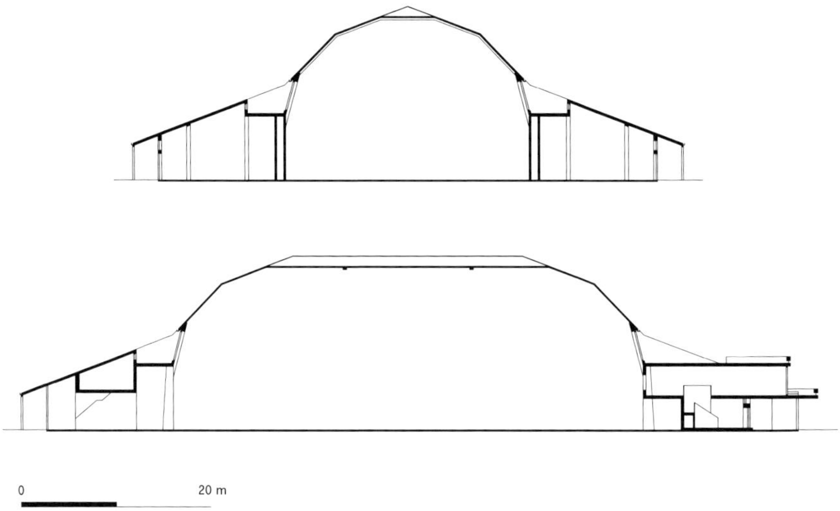

1959–60

ROBERTO GABETTI, AIMARO ISOLA

RIDING HALL

TURIN, NICHELINO, VIA DEI CACCIATORI, VIALE CIBRARIO

At its completion, the riding hall of the *Società Ippica Torinese* had no immediate neighbors; at present it is wedged between a shopping center and a highway. Seen from the exterior the building appears to be a huge tent—this impression is created by the striking roof and its distinctive folds and cutouts. The riding club's rooms are all united under the large roof: the hall itself is in the middle of the central floor plan. The auxiliary spaces—horse stalls, hay storage and break rooms—surround it. The outermost layer is a covered walkway that runs the entire perimeter of the building. The slender exterior columns hint at a free-flowing space inside the building. In fact, the opposite is the case: the riding hall is a focused, vaulted space.

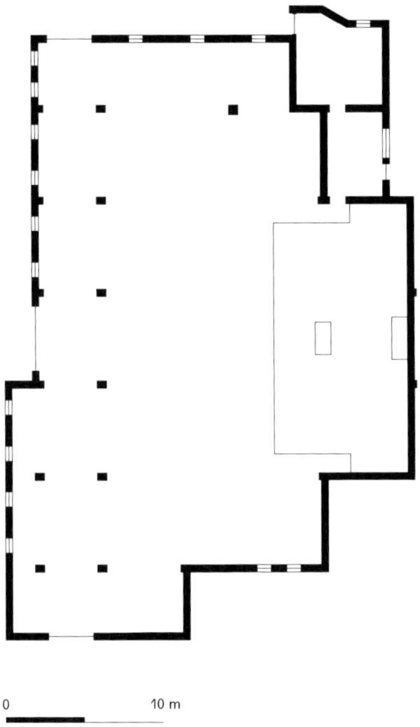

1959–61

GIOVANNI MICHELUCCI

CHIESA DEL CUORE IMMACOLATO DI MARIA
PISTOIA, VILLAGGIO BELVEDERE, VIALE DEI TIGLI 40

This church is located on the edge of Pistoia, next to the Villaggio Belvedere residential complex [→**108**], which is why it is also referred to as Chiesa del Belvedere. In Michelucci's prolific body of work, the design of churches played a significant role from the very beginning. The earlier churches were characterized by axiality of the longitudinal nave. In this project he moved away from that conventional configuration and developed a tent-like worship space with the altar placed on one of the long sides. Reinforced concrete columns and buttresses pass through the space; white ceilings—reminiscent of tent fabric—are suspended between them. The unusual structural concept is visible in the elevations: stained-glass windows are inserted between the concrete buttresses. The walls are in ashlar stone.

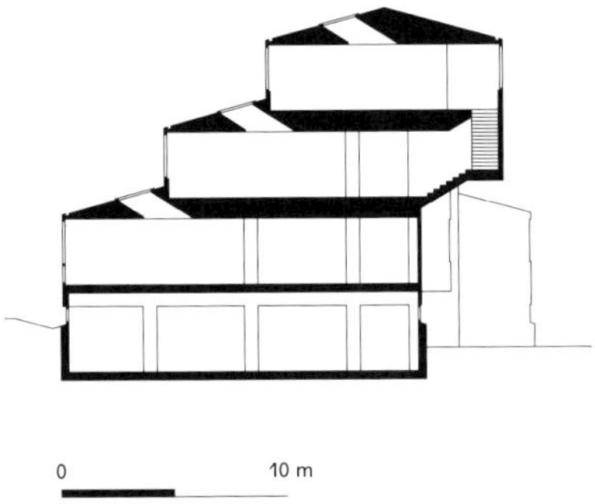

1959–61

GINO VALLE

ZANUSSI OFFICE BUILDING
PORCIA, CORSO LINO ZANUSSI

Gino Valle had a long, productive relationship with Zanussi, a manufacturer of household appliances. He designed several complexes, warehouses, and a cafeteria for the company. This office building in Porcia functions both as screen and as gateway to the factory grounds: the top level projects beyond the facade and bridges the vehicle entrance. It seems as if the linear building could press on indefinitely—and Valle also developed plans for an extension on the other side of the gateway. In his design, Valle emphasized the building's load-bearing members. He employed broad piers and brackets, and integrated stairways in the cantilever. The exposed concrete elevation facing the street contrasts with the extensively glazed facade, which steps down toward the factory. Oblique skylights are cut out of the ceilings.

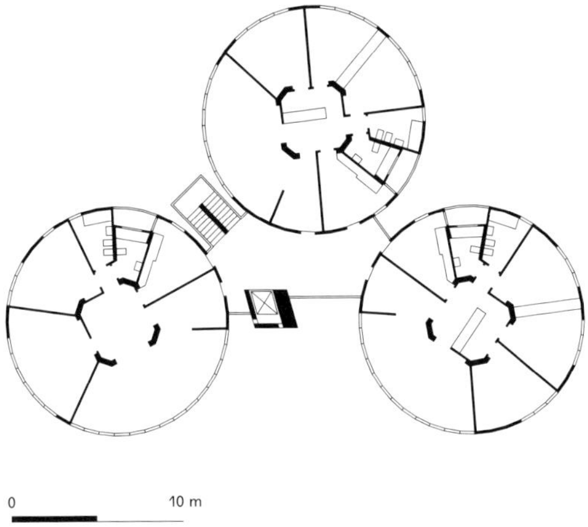

1959–62

ANGELO MANGIAROTTI, BRUNO MORASSUTTI

APARTMENT BUILDING
MILAN, VIA GAVIRATE 27

This unorthodox structure on a broad boulevard has—quite aptly—been dubbed the Three-Cylinder Building. Its drums are linked only by the stairwell in the space between them. As so often in their designs, Mangiarotti & Morassutti paid special attention to structural aspects: each cylinder rests on a single pier. The ground level is open to the elements, revealing the silhouette of the mushroom piers. On the upper levels the loads are distributed via floors that cantilever out from reinforced concrete cores. Consequently, the other walls in the apartments have no structural function. The column-free exterior walls are sheathed in prefabricated panels made either of glass or of wood.

1959–63

LUIGI CACCIA DOMINIONI

APARTMENT BUILDING
MAILAND, VIA ANDREA MASSENA 18

The ten-story block located on the edge of Giardino Valentino Bompiani has a bi-partite structure: the half of the building facing the park is distinguished by balconies, floor-to-ceiling glazing, shutters and stucco walls. Caccia Dominioni's detailing of the other half draws on a design of an orphanage [→**18**] that he began working on in 1948: the facade is composed of hexagonal tiles and hexagonal brick grilles. Despite this formal dichotomy, through his color scheme the architect attained a homogeneous overall impression. The apartment building's ceramic skin extends all the way to the ground: there is no separate base detail.

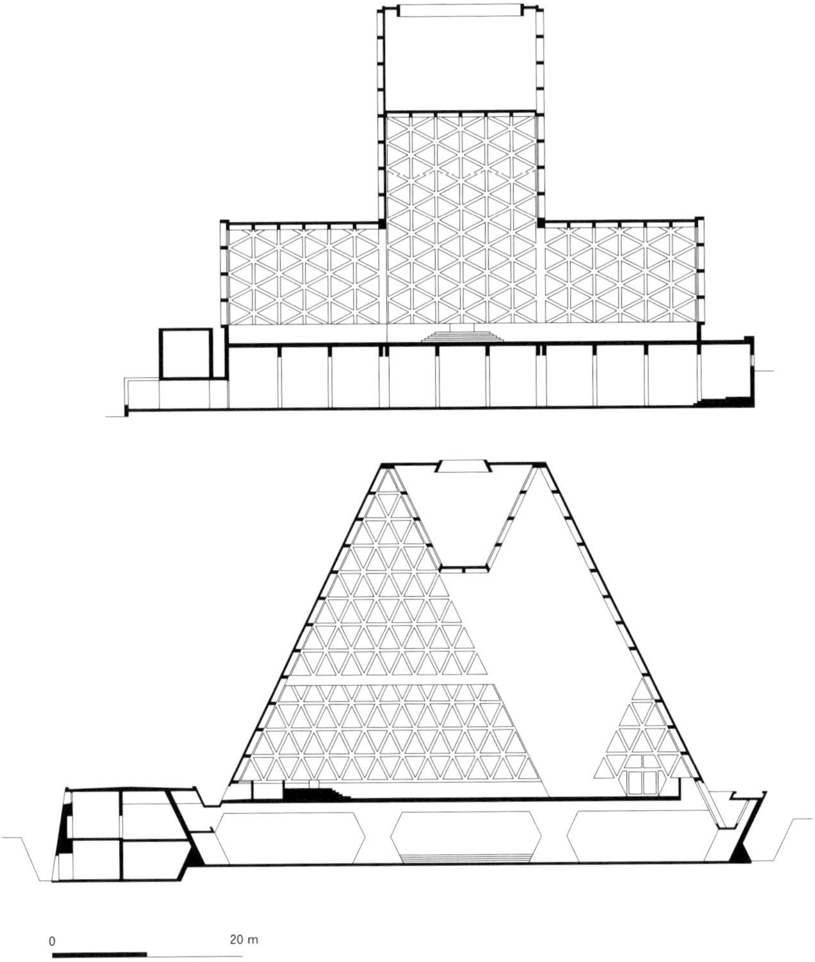

ANTONIO GUACCI

SANTUARIO DI MONTE GRISA
TRIESTE, PROSECCO

1959–66

In 1945, Bishop Antonio Satin made a vow to erect a church if Trieste were to survive the war. The first preparations toward the realization of this church were undertaken by Umberto Nordio. Adalberto Libera and Luigi Moretti were also involved as consultants. The design that was ultimately built was the work of Antonio Guacci. He was interested in the development of ornamental concepts originating in circles, triangles, spheres and cylinders. The commission atop Monte Grisa finally gave him the opportunity to build one of his geometric "utopias." The unusual task and the dramatic location on a plateau with a view of the sea allowed him to stay very close to his fantastical drawings.

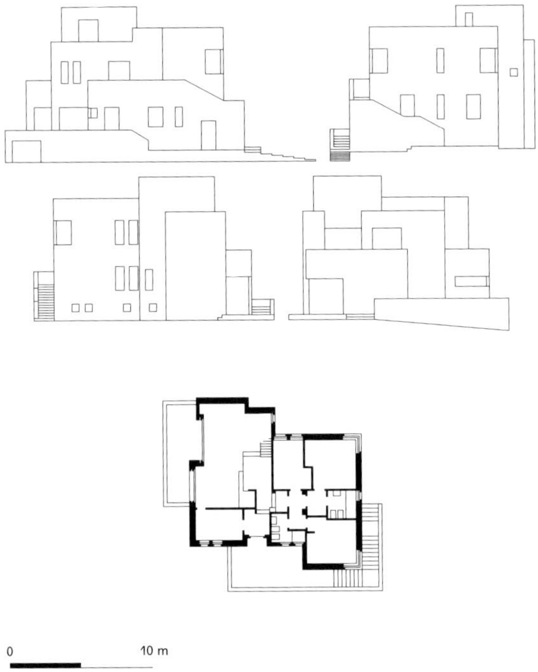

1960

ALDO ROSSI
HOLIDAY HOME
MARINA DI MASSA, LOCALITÀ RONCHI, VIA FICHI

Less than a kilometer from the sea, a narrow alley through a pine grove leads to a structure with two units, each with its own entrance. An exterior stair leads to the unit occupying the upper level. This was the very first of Aldo Rossi's projects to be realized. After completing his degree, he worked for *Casabella*. In 1959, the magazine published an issue dedicated to the work of Adolf Loos (*Casabella* № 233). Rossi's essay testifies to his considerable knowledge of Loos's work. This is also evident in the design of the house in Massa: it's almost as if, following Giuseppe de Finetti—who studied in Vienna from 1913 to 1915—Rossi had somehow managed to become the second Italian to study architecture with Loos.

LEONARDO RICCI

OFFICE BUILDING

MASSA, PIAZZA ARANCI, VIA CAVOUR

Occupying a trapezoidal site in the center of Massa, this office building consists of two distinct parts: a restrained half facing Piazza Aranci (opposite Palazzo Ducale) and a spectacular half on the property's narrow end. The third floor projects beyond the others and holds the two parts together; to emphasize the horizontality, the ceiling height of this level is reduced at the edges. The design is characterized by the interplay of horizontal and vertical elements—this is especially evident in the treatment of the narrow end: volumes of various heights and widths are stacked adeptly, almost as if they were separate buildings designed by different architects.

1960

COMITATO ELETTORALE
ENRICO ROSSI

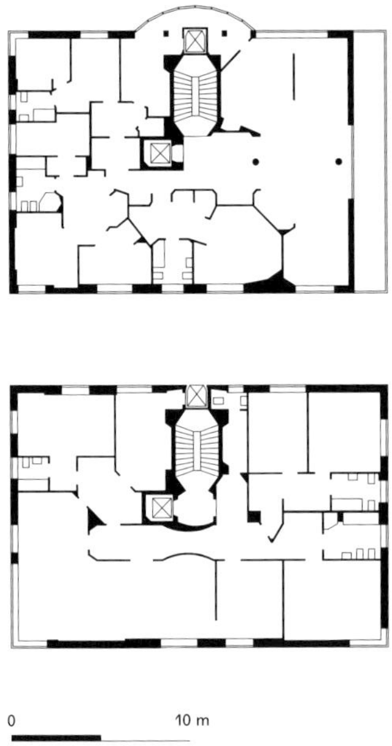

1960–61

LUIGI CACCIA DOMINIONI

APARTMENT BUILDING
MILAN, PIAZZA CARBONARI 2

Caccia Dominioni's design is a variation on the theme of the structure on Via Nievo [→**68**]. It seems as if it is a segment cut from a long extrusion. The roof zone is trimmed back as specified by the building code. The building contains condominiums: there is one unit per level, and the floor plans were designed in accordance with the wishes of the respective owners. The reinforced concrete frame structure allowed the architect to develop a variety of spaces and spatial sequences. The reflective ceramic facade showcases Caccia Dominioni's adeptness at incorporating different window formats and types of solar control. Sliding shutters are stored behind black glazed panels, and roller blinds are integrated in the windows' lintels.

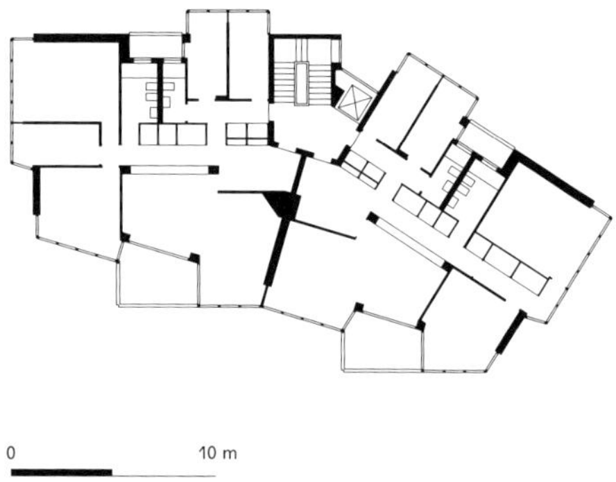

1960–62

ANGELO MANGIAROTTI, BRUNO MORASSUTTI

APARTMENT BUILDING
MILAN, VIA QUADRONNO 24

This freestanding, tower-like apartment building is at once Miesian and expressionist. The duo devised the finely composed overall form—containing rooms with high ceilings—and the Three-Cylinder Building [→**136**] in quick succession. But in this case the load-bearing structure is more conventional: it consists of a reinforced concrete frame and shear walls. But both projects employ prefabricated facade panels of wood—in this case they are more than three meters high and made of Douglas fir. The building's floor plan is asymmetrical and has several ins and outs. There are two units per level, each with a separate entrance for the household staff. The floor plans vary from level to level. This is evident in the different arrangements of the glass and wood panels on the side facing the park.

ISTITUTO ORTOPEDICO

1960–63

LUIGI CACCIA DOMINIONI

CONVENTO DI SAN ANTONIO FRATI MINORI
MILAN, VIA CARLO FARINI 10

Caccia Dominioni first used brick grilles to structure the building envelope in his design of an orphanage; the grilles extend—like a frieze—the entire width of the facade [→**18**]. For the convent depicted here, he designed a consummate brick-grille tower, in which the ornamental loggia cutouts are the constitutive element. The tower displays the classical facade configuration: there is differentiation of the top and the base. The lowermost loggias have closed parapets; this additional mass gives the building a solid base. The cutouts on the next six stories are identical, but Caccia Dominioni modifies the motif on the top floor: here, there are six window axes instead of three, and the openings are smaller both in height and width.

The first church space [→74]: a roof slab of finely wrought concrete elements, floating, at first glance, there appear to be no columns, atop floor-to-ceiling glass walls; red ceramic floor, delicate stacking chairs. Upon closer inspection you see that the photo is positioned such that the two concrete columns to the right and left of the altar are not immediately recognizable because they coincide visually with the vertical subdivisions of the glass walls. Indeed, the four slender concrete columns support a roof of the same material, thought through with respect to the flow of forces and detailing—a baldachin concept; the vertical envelope tends toward "nothing but light," light filtered by walls of matt glass. Conventional spatial iconography of the clerical sort is missing. It is an abstract, universal, translucent place—and it immediately brings to mind the spatial and structural logic of Ludwig Mies van der Rohe: roof—columns—incorporeal wall. But Mies would have made the ceiling neutral, abstract and non-directional.

What else do we see? A startling aging process, the glass in the walls, or more precisely, the insulating material, is rotting, the concrete grimly darkened and soiled, the visible sacred objects a bit foreign, strewn about awkwardly. Nevertheless, the space as a whole is currently in use. We instinctively conflate it with the visions for church design in Austria around 1957/58—the project by *Arbeitsgruppe 4* for the St. Florian Church in Vienna, and the pastoral center in Steyr/Ennsleiten by Johann Georg Gsteu and *Arbeitsgruppe 4* realized shortly thereafter. We recall that from 1953 to 1954, Angelo Mangiarotti, who designed the church in question, taught at the IIT in Chicago, which, at the time, was headed by Mies van der Rohe in his

MANFREDO TAFURI, FRANCESCO DAL CO: *HISTORY OF WORLD ARCHITECTURE. MODERN ARCHITECTURE*. NEW YORK 1986, P. 261
(First published in Italian in 1976)
As in the case of Persico, the activities of Olivetti helped to weld the positions of antifascism to those of the postwar culture outside the intermediary of official Policy. His utopias, paternalism, and patriarchal socialism exerted a fascination over Italian postwar culture, which looked to "the island of Ivrea" as myth and goal. On the model of that "republic of letters and social peace" would be shaped one component of architectural thinking ready to lay down its arms before any power disposed to flatter it. If Persico is the symbol of the obstinate faith of the Catholic culture that, in the technocratic apparatus of fascism, was preparing its own return to the fore, Olivetti deserves credit for having launched an organic project for a "corporate state of culture," matrix of the third force of the architectural and town-planning intelligentsia after 1945.

most productive American phase, and where, after working with Gropius, Konrad Wachsmann became a professor. During Wachsmann's time in Chicago, he forged new paths with his hangar designs for the United States Air Force. In the nineteen-sixties, Mangiarotti also became an important point of reference for the Viennese scene gathered around *Arbeitsgruppe 4*, Puchhammer/Wawrik, Hiesmayr and Schwanzer, among others. They were trying to renew architecture by making use of prefabrication construction processes. In 1965, Olivetti (!) presented a Mangiarotti exhibition at its Vienna headquarters, and Hermann Czech wrote a lucid review of it ...

The second church space [→133]: here too the elaborate concrete structure is at the center—yet the stance and mood are entirely different. The load-bearing concrete structure is highly specific, set up gesturally, and tells a story that is easy to understand, but not simplistic: its myriad facets engage in an exciting, equitable dialogue with other contrasting materials. The large "trees," "crosses," "masts," or "parasols" that splay the space reach out with their booms and branches to a wall system of solid, archaic stone masonry. They frame glass walls, partially of stained glass, and large windows, and support a textile-like, light, bright, vaulted membrane ceiling. Reddish ceramic floor like before. What catches your attention in this photo in contrast to the preceding photo: the building is in perfect condition and is a drastic inversion of conventional spatial orchestration of churches—the vertexes of the space are "above the congregation," and the spatial dynamics decrease toward the altar. The light comes "from behind." It flows, in other words, to the front indirectly and evenly above the congregation. This church was well published in its day. The architect, Giovanni Michelucci,

HERMANN CZECH: *ANGELO MANGIAROTTI (1965)*, IN: ZUR ABWECHSLUNG. AUSGEWÄHLTE SCHRIFTEN ZUR ARCHITEKTUR. WIEN. VIENNA 1977, PP. 47–48

(Reprint of a review of the Mangiarotti exhibition shown in Vienna in 1965, published in *Die Furche*)

In the works of Mangiarotti, the sort of reserve that leaves part of the decisions to the consumer is refuted, not only theoretically, but also through material evidence. His prefabricated structural components have an elegance that cannot stay neutral. But this elegance—the elegance of industrial design—also indicates that level of reflection at which the structural problem is resolved, making the technical venture a thing of the past. And in the land of Josef Hoffmann, one must ask why someone with the will to be graceful would not dispense with the professed reasoning and leave structure out of it.

This hints at the difficulties that stand in the way of a direct influence of this architecture. The very person who expects impulses from technology will be skeptical of the *Werkbund* mind-set that wants to ennoble the technical object, of a formal later became famous for another religious space, the much more expressive "highway church" outside Florence (completed in 1961).

This was the first modern Italian building I experienced in situ—it was on a trip through Italy in 1968 with a childhood friend, in his Citroën 2CV, with soft top and horizontal gear shift. We took an hour-long break there. I made drawings of the space inside and outside. The virtuosity of the concrete forms was impressive, exuberant, and could quickly be depicted in pencil and charcoal. But next to the Autostrada del Sole in "no-man's-land," there seemed to me to be no convincing explanation for this act of violence. Michelucci had an enormous, interesting oeuvre that went back farther, but it didn't really interest us ignorant, long-haired revolutionaries. In the late nineteen-seventies, he was "rediscovered" as a pioneering contextualist, thanks above all to an important exhibition at the Technical University of Munich entitled *Neues Bauen in alter Umgebung* (New Construction in Old Settings), the brainchild of Fritz Kurrent.

Third concrete study, the next escalation, the photo [→103] only captures part of it: the freedom of concrete in fantastic exuberance; unlike Michelucci, no longer told as precise "history," legible, and "breached" by the regional material, but rather an entirely subjective, autonomous sculpture, free of functional, formal, typological or economical rationality; again a baldachin of sorts, yet contrary to Mangiarotti's formal and material discipline; including an equally animated, glass-wall cascade—bizarre, grandiose. And what's it all for? That can't be a church!? Perhaps a museum? A cultural center? No, it's a primary school in the architect's hometown halfway between Milan and Lago Maggiore; and when one asks who the architect is, the answer causes

beauty that robs the structure of its sobriety and acerbity. But will a person impressed precisely by the form not imitate at an inferior level and seek technical reasons for ornamentation? What remains is just appreciation for the high quality—of a kind that finds no match in talent here.

ALDO ROSSI: *A SCIENTIFIC AUTOBIOGRAPHY*. CAMBRIDGE, MASSACHUSETTS / LONDON 1981, P. 46
All things considered, Giulio Argan's book on Gropius was a beautiful romance, but it was not concerned with facts. My favorite book was certainly that of Loos, which I read and studied on the recommendation of a man whom I should also call my mentor, Ernesto N. Rogers. I read Loos for the first time around 1959 in the beautiful first edition published by Brenner Verlag and given to me by Rogers. Perhaps this architect alone revealed the connection to the great questions: the Austrian and German tradition of Fischer von Erlach and Schinkel, local culture, handicrafts, history, and especially

consternation: Castiglioni! Aren't those the brothers with the wry, minimalist, incredibly intelligent, witty yet unwieldy, incorporeal design objects for Zanotta, Artemide, Flos? No, a different one. Enrico Castiglioni, a major figure in the mid-sixties, now completely forgotten ...

TENTH NOTE, ACTUALLY APPENDIX TO NINTH NOTE

The view of the Olivetti training center in Ivrea [→263] already fascinated me three years ago when Martin Feiersinger showed me a small selection of these Italomodern photos. We see here how a stupendously detailed machine-building, organized and stacked to an extreme, arches over the terrain and collides with the old urban substance typical of northern Italy.

Moreover, in the foreground there are large trees and park-like vegetation. The building is like an artificial cataract. It reveals the tendencies that were prevalent in the late sixties: flexible large structures with clip-on or plug-in systems, on top of that, the detail, material and color nuances of those years in which architecture sought to fully integrate plastics technology, pop art colors, and the aesthetics of operable, machine-like building components. Still more, the facility reflects the presence of small, individual cells in a large, spatially and functionally complex collective structure. In comparison to the buildings discussed above, the origin of the structural/technological vehemence here is not primarily architectural, but essentially influenced by the product design of the boom years.

I wasn't familiar with the building—nor with the architects, because in 1975/76, when it opened, my interest was focused elsewhere, and this Olivetti building—comparable to the Centre Pompidou (by the Italian

theater and poetry. Without doubt I owe to this reading of Loos the profound contempt I have always felt for industrial design and for the confounding of form and function. Through Loos I discovered Kraus, Schoenberg, Wittgenstein, and above all, Trakl, but also the great architecture of ancient Rome and an America which I would come to understand only much later. I read about all these subjects and artists perhaps in an ingenuous way, but this may have been the only way to do such reading. It has long gained me the reputation of being a Germanophile.

ROSSI, OP. CIT., PP. 15–16

Around 1960 I wrote *The Architecture of the City*, a successful book. At that time, I was not yet thirty years old, and as I have said, I wanted to write a definitive work: it seemed to me that everything, once clarified, could be defined. I believed that the Renaissance treatise had to become an apparatus which could be translated into objects. I scorned memories, and at the same time, I made use of urban impressions: behind feelings

& British/Italian team Renzo Piano & Richard Rogers, a great-nephew of Ernesto N. Rogers), which opened the following year—is something of a "high" and "late" work of the "technoid" genre. With indoor pool, auditorium, conference rooms, and cinema, with living units designed through and through like motor homes or luxurious convertibles; one segment employs enormous pre-tensioned concrete beams to span over Roman ruins.

The ensemble was intended as an urban catalyst for Ivrea's central business district, but, as Feiersinger relates, none of it worked: before construction was completed the training center was re-planned to function as a hotel. Olivetti unhappily owned the complex until 1996; it has been empty since. Despite its artistic magnificence, the concerns regarding its building physics and maintenance, as well as its functionalist exaggeration, reflect the crisis, beginning in the nineteen-eighties, of the Italian architecture and design miracle, in general, and its lodestar, the firm Olivetti, in particular.

In the nineteen-twenties in the Piedmontese city of Ivrea, a company for the production of office machines, calculators and computers headed by Camillo and Adriano Olivetti began with 200 employees; prior to the Second World War it grew into an innovation- and design-conscious typewriter brand and resisted all of fascism's advances. Beginning in 1936, it groomed the best young architects and industrial designers—Figini & Pollini, Studio BBPR, Marcello Nizzoli. After 1950, it became global leader of the branch, erected in Ivrea a business empire in the sense of a vision of a "socialism without Marx," and around 1970 commissioned Carlo Scarpa, Louis Kahn,

I searched for the fixed laws of a timeless typology. I saw courts and galleries, the elements of urban morphology, distributed in the city with the purity of mineralogy. I read books on urban geography, topography, and history, like a general who wishes to know every possible battlefield—the high grounds, the passages, the woods. I walked the cities of Europe to understand their plans and classify them according to types. Like a lover sustained by my egotism, I often ignored the secret feelings I had for those cities; it was enough to know the system that governed them. Perhaps I simply wanted to free myself of the city. Actually, I was discovering my own architecture. A confusion of courtyards, suburban houses, roofs, gas storage drums, comprised my first exploration of Milan that seemed fantastic to me.

Kenzo Tange, BBPR, James Stirling, Ignazio Gardella, Gae Aulenti, Marco Zanuso, Egon Eiermann, Richard Meier and the designers Ettore Sottsass, Mario Bellini in Italy and abroad ...

A personal remark on Olivetti's design icon named *Valentine*—an ultra-light, bright-red typewriter with rounded edges and plastic case designed in 1969 by Sottsass: I wrote the first texts for Missing Link, then for *UMBAU* and later, for the weekend features section of *Die Presse* on an Underwood—black, metallic, weighing several kilograms—that had been given to me. My girlfriend (later to become my wife) had a *Valentine*, and when I visited her, for example, while she was travelling or studying in Rome or Paris, I typed on the *Valentine*. She still has it—it's stowed away for a rainy day ...

In 1977, an interview of Ettore Sottsass accompanied an article in a German journal on the training center in Ivrea. He already distanced himself from all of the technoid product, consumer and societal ideologies. As one of the father figures of the Italian *Radical Design* of the next generation, he played a decisive role in determining the change of course toward postmodernism in the design of buildings and products, which, in the activities of *Global Tools*, *Alchimia,* and *Memphis*, again made northern Italy a trendsetter until the early nineteen-eighties.

ELEVENTH NOTE

Reflections on the art of building in the twentieth century between Italy and Austria, between *Pianeta Milano* and *Pianeta Vienna*, go back a long time, typically focused on individuals, grouped around the pertinent professional media and forums. My own experiences with congenial

PIER PAOLO PASOLINI: OPEN LETTER TO ITALO CALVINO, IN: *PAESE SERA*, "LETTERA APERTA A ITALO CALVINO: PASOLINI: QUELLO CHE RIMPIANGO," 8 JULY 1974
Dear Calvino! Maurizio Ferrara says that I mourn a "Golden Age." You say that I mourn Good Old Italy": everyone says that I mourn something, and by giving this mourning a negative connotation they turn it into a target that is easy to hit ... The people of this universe neither experienced a "Golden Age" nor did they have anything to do with "Good Old Italy." They lived in the age that Chilanti named the *Age of Bread*. They were consumers of indispensable goods. Perhaps that was what made their poor and precarious life necessary. It is clear that superfluous goods make life superfluous (to sum up in elementary terms) ... I have claimed and I repeat: the cultural permeation of the world by a consumption-oriented, all-assimilating center has destroyed the different cultures of the Third World (I am still speaking here at the global scale and therefore am also referring to the cultures of the Third World that essentially correspond to Italy's peasant culture). Just a single cultural model is offered to the Italians (and, by the way,

protagonists in Italy who, on average, were several years older than me, dated to the period from 1971 to 1977. The scene around that time and thereafter—*Superstudio*, *UFO*, and *Archizoom*—was indeed very different from the circumstances in Vienna. The leftist revolutionaries Adolfo Natalini, Gianni Pettena, Alessandro Mendini and their numerous theoretical exegetes seemed to have it all—with the best connections to the large global firms, navigating an excellent, internationally oriented, journalistic context.

Aside from the leading media such as *Domus*, *Casabella*, *Rassegna*, *L'architettura*, *Lotus*, which were already taking part at the forefront of the debates, the "alternative" and autonomous, even more broadly conceived transdisciplinary formats such as *Controspazio*, *Modo*, *IN* and *INPIÙ* arose; the variety and excitement, the rhetorical fervor, emphasis on pleasure and the acuity of the discourse elicited the comparison to Austrian architectural journalism. Here in Vienna from 1965 to 1969, there was only *Der Bau*, a concise medium that, both with respect to aesthetics and content, was *au courant*, yet completely "pure," not linked to business interests, domestic product design, nor to the movements and conflicts at university and professional levels. In the nineteen-seventies there was nothing left like it. But in Italy that all (apparently?) happened in the thick of things, in flux, the focal point of refined everyday culture, which promised to soon become mainstream.

When, following a long discussion—taxing with regard to both content and my language skills—of Bruno Kreisky's politics, Mendini and Mosoni explained to me that the standard of living was much higher in Milan and

to all the people on earth). The adaptation to this model takes place above all in a person's body and demeanor. Here the values of the new culture of the consumption civilization are already being lived out, that means, of the new and most repressive totalitarianism ever known to man—even if these values have not yet found complete expression. From the standpoint of verbal expression, the entire language is reduced to a language of pronouncements: a terrible impoverishment of expression occurs. The dialects (the mother tongues!) have receded—both with respect to time and place—into the distance: the sons are forced to no longer speak them because they live in Turin, Milan or in Germany. Where they are still spoken they have lost their inventive potential. A boy from the suburbs of Rome would not be able to understand, for example, the dialect of the novels I wrote ten or fifteen years ago. In a twist of fate, like a respectable citizen from the north, he would have to use the glossary appended to it.

in northern Italy than in Vienna, I ultimately had to, reluctantly and fairly ignorantly, agree. At the time, Mendini already drove an Alfa Romeo—and hadn't built anything yet. In 1975, I didn't even own a bicycle.

TWELFTH NOTE

Beginning in 1976/77, I discovered the larger story of the Milan–Vienna connection by way of a renewed orientation toward tangible architecture projects embarked upon with Adolf Krischanitz, and in our post-university studies of Austrian modernism. In addition to that, there was my involvement in the *Österreichische Gesellschaft für Architektur*, an architecture organization whose board had just taken on new members of a younger generation—Dietmar Steiner, Paul Katzberger, Margarethe Cufer, Sonja Gasparin and others (who at the time were still working on their theses at the Academy of Fine Arts on Schillerplatz) actively sought out contacts in Ticino, in Basel and in Zurich. On account of the lattermost's Lugano–Como–Milan–Venice axis and, above all, Aldo Rossi, the perspective shifted from trans-Atlantic to trans-Alpine continuities ...

From 1920 to 1952, Giuseppe de Finetti—who had studied under Adolf Loos—worked in Milan and built well-crafted and spatially "polished" residences and interiors; prepared numerous urban-planning studies and projects; and published articles in daily newspapers and in professional journals, including in 1934 in *Casabella* his Italian translation of Loos's text "Ornament and Crime." Beginning in 1931, the young Edoardo Persico published trenchant reviews of the work of Loos and Hoffmann in *Casabella*. At the 5th Triennale in Milan, Loos was presented as one of the pioneering

TAFURI, DAL CO: OP. CIT., P. 296
Despite a few other measures put into effect sector by sector, there followed a period in which the aberrant mechanism that had traditionally characterized the Italian situation were reinforced. Land was left in the hands of speculators, while low-rent housing ventures dropped to a ridiculous percentage of the whole. Corruption ran rampant in the municipal administrations; the great real estate concentrations together with widespread petty speculation permanently defaced the cities: and the deterioration in hydrogeological resources became no less grave than the deterioration of the cities themselves. All this was made even more dramatic by a series of appalling natural disasters. On July 19, 1966, an entire portion of the city of Agrigento collapsed under the weight of thousands of rooms built without proper authorizations and controls. On November 4 of the same year the waters of the Arno River poured over Florence, and the old bastions of the *Serenissima* proved insufficient to protect Venice from a flood of fearful dimensions. The most admired cities of Italy paid a very heavy toll for

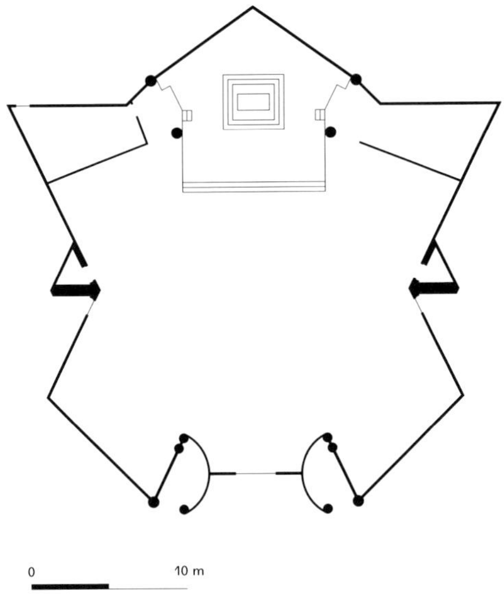

GIUSEPPE PIZZIGONI

CHIESA SANTA MARIA IMMACOLATA
BERGAMO, LONGUELO, VIA MATTIOLI 57

1960–63

During the late nineteen-fifties Pizzigoni carried out several experiments with thin concrete shells, including small-scale structures for his own use. The design of this church in Bergamo—an irrational and exploratory building that posed considerable challenges with respect to both geometry and structure—results directly from these tests. The building is made up of a structural frame in the form of linear concrete members joined at every imaginable angle and a six-centimeter-thick concrete skin. This yields a complex spatial give-and-take between the load-bearing skeleton—visible both inside and outside the church—and the shell in its various incarnations as draped, stretched, vaulted or overlapping skin. Pizzigoni's decision to work with a symmetrical floor plan is puzzling and detracts from the experience of the remarkable space.

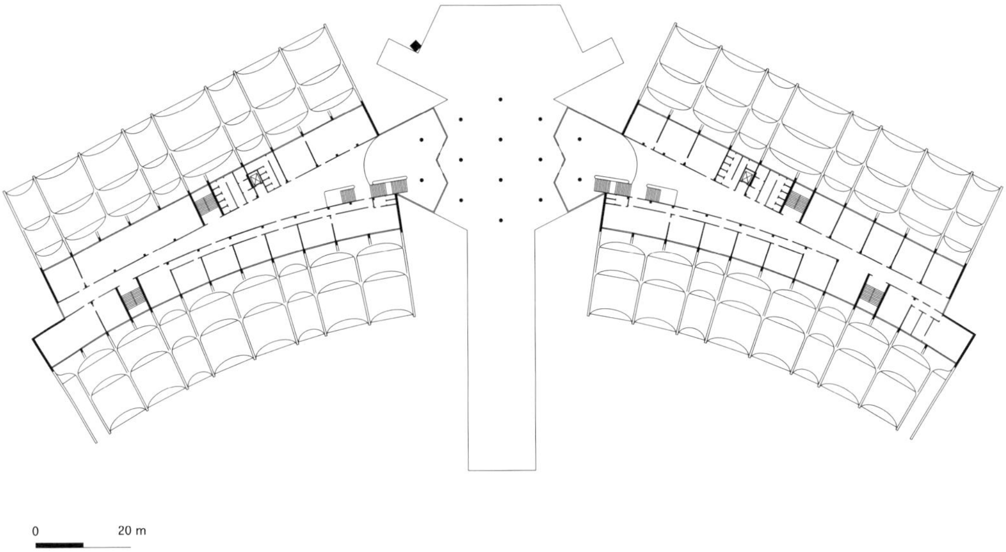

ENRICO CASTIGLIONI

ISTITUTO TECNICO INDUSTRIALE E ISTITUTO PROFESSIONALE DI STATO
BUSTO ARSIZIO, CASTELLANZA, VIA AZZIMONTI

1960–64

Castiglioni's vocational school in Busto Arsizio is an expressive building radiating the robustness and rawness associated with brutalism. A broad ramp—underneath it is the school's gymnasium—leads to the symmetrical complex's raised, covered forecourt. The entrances to the separate wings are on both sides of this forecourt. Lofty training workshops are located in the basement. Seen from the exterior, their low-slung concrete-shell roofs give the false impression that the workshops below must have low ceilings because at first glance the floor is assumed to be at ground level.

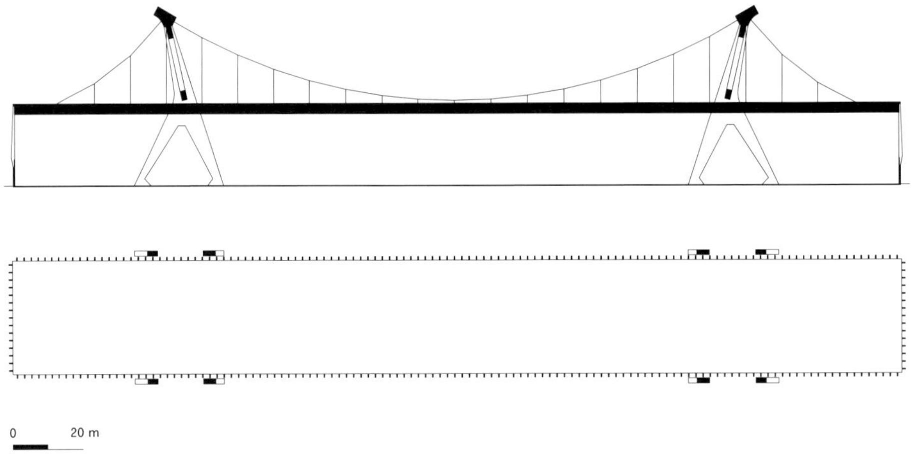

1960–64

PIER LUIGI NERVI

PAPER FACTORY
MANTUA, VIA POGGIO REALE 9

Pier Luigi Nervi, one of the most important structural engineers of the twentieth century, constructed a surprisingly small number of bridges. His design of a paper factory on the edge of Mantua, however, is indebted to bridge construction; immediately following its completion, it was described in the July 1964 issue of *Architectural Forum* as a "factory with the grace of a bridge." The decision to develop a bridge-like structure was based not only on aesthetic considerations, but also on the functional requirements: the building envelope shelters a huge paper machine, and the roof is suspended from the cable-stayed structure. The free span between the pylons measures one hundred sixty meters and the hall is thirty meters wide. Consequently, it would be no exaggeration to call it Nervi's most stunning bridge.

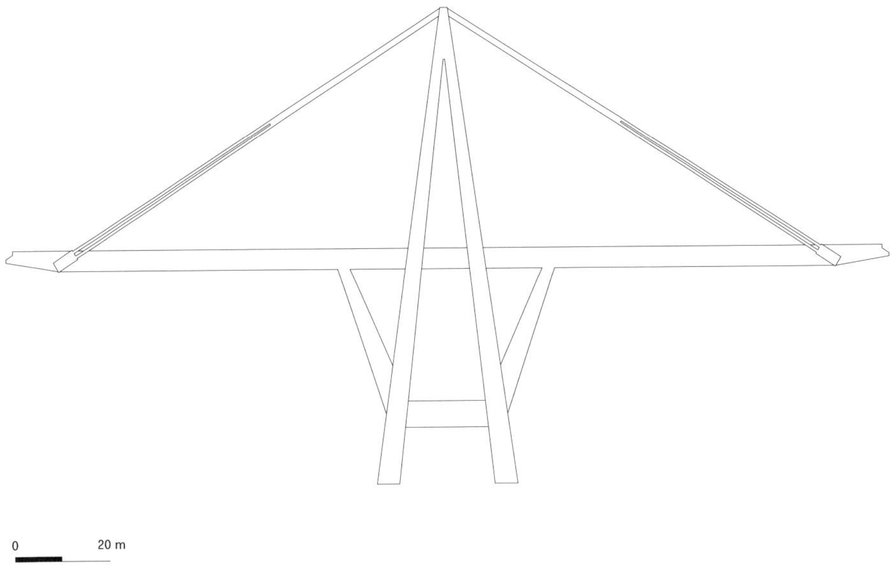

1960–67

RICCARDO MORANDI

HIGHWAY BRIDGE
GENOA, VIADOTTO SUL POLCEVERA, A10 GENUA-SAVONA

This bridge was constructed above apartment buildings, industrial compounds and a railroad yard. Morandi employed three identical pylons where the longest spans were required. Their presence in the urban fabric has the feel of expressive, gigantic sculptures. The realization of a suspended structure employing pre-tensioned concrete was a considerable challenge. Morandi was a pioneer in this domain: by 1948, he had already patented a pre-tensioning method bearing his name. Two of the pylons are still in the original state. The concrete stays of the third have been retrofitted with steel cables on the concrete's surface [→**172**].

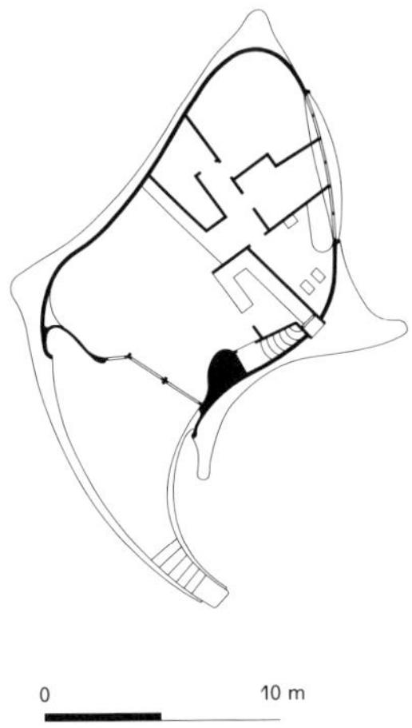

VITTORIO GIORGINI

HOLIDAY HOME

BARATTI

1961–62

In 1957, on a wooded patch of land near his Hexagon House [→**96**], Giorgini began to explore the possibilities of thin, zoomorphic concrete shells. These studies set the stage for this holiday home—referred to as The Whale—located just a stone's throw from them. The design of this structure as an inhabitable sculpture bears witness to Giorgini's search for alternative ways of building. The flowing forms are also reminiscent of the thin shells reinforced with chicken wire that Frederick Kiesler experimented with in his Endless House. Nonetheless, when asked about influences on his work, Giorgioni pointed to nature as the most important source of inspiration. As related to us by the gardener, years ago there were goldfish in the shallow freeform pool that surrounds the stair and follows the contour of the shell's lower edge.

N M 1:5000

1961–63

LUIGI CACCIA DOMINIONI

HOLIDAY HOMES

PINETA DI ARENZANO, VIA DELLA ROTONDA

In 1958, Luigi Caccia Dominioni and Ignazio Gardella began work on a master plan for the Belvedere, a colony of weekend homes in Pineta di Arenzano. The two architects developed two strikingly different settlements right next to each other; Gardella inserted his structures in the cliff [→**124**], and Caccia Dominioni placed a group of citadel-like, freestanding structures on the plateau. The latter are scattered throughout the lush, park-like topography. No ordering principle is evident. Their exteriors hark back to a different era. Instead of the dark tiles that are a hallmark of his Milanese facades, here Caccia Dominioni chose light hues of stucco. Following the completion of this ensemble, he began work on San Martino (1963–64), the community's church [→**183**]; it was designed in the same vein as his other structures.

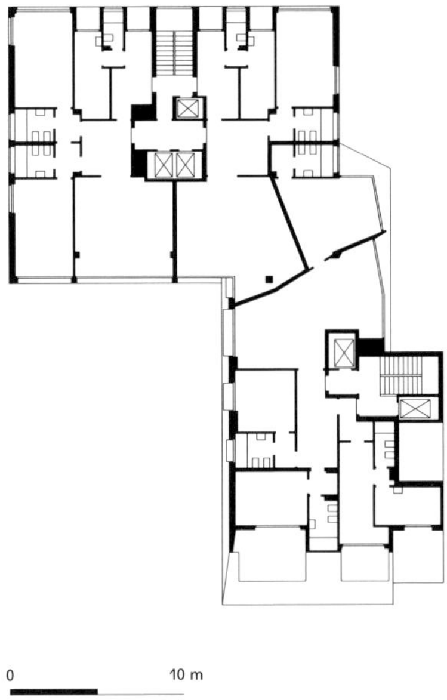

1961–64

MARIO ASNAGO, CLAUDIO VENDER

MIXED-USE BUILDING
MILAN, VIA ANDREA VERGA 4

Urbanistically speaking, this project marks the transition from fabric with continuous frontage to freestanding structures. On the side of the building facing the street, three of the seven stories are integrated in the mansard roof. The latter is screened from the sidewalk, and only the first of the three levels has slanted walls. Above it the roof cloaks the terraces, which step back from the street. Toward the garden forecourt, however, the roof is so steep that the windows are distributed as if it were a facade. Only the materiality makes it recognizable as a roof: in contrast to the facades, which are clad in travertine, the roof has a copper surface. As depicted in the photo, where the two parts of the building intersect, the windows were cut out of both walls. Thus, the living rooms have views in two directions.

M 1:5000

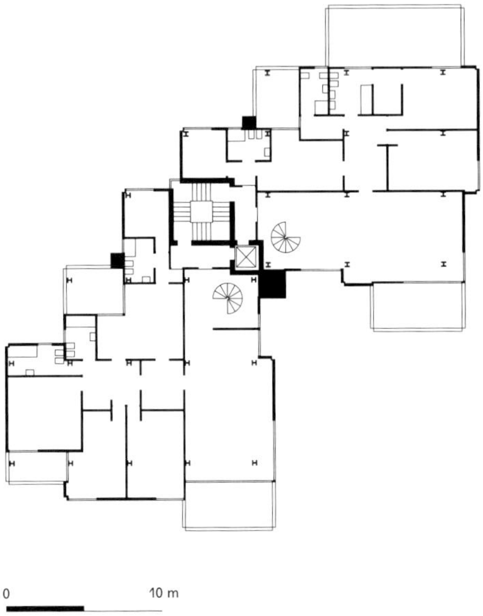

1961–64

MARCO ZANUSO

APARTMENT BUILDINGS

MILAN, VIA LAVENO 6

These twin structures clad in stone make a hefty, solid first impression. But the ground level's thin columns tell another story: the structures are supported by slender steel members, and only the cores holding the stairs and lifts make use of reinforced concrete. The assembly of the outer walls consists of prefabricated, six-centimeter-thick metal panels, an air layer, and a facade of three-centimeter-thick sheets of stone mounted on aluminum profiles. The notched upper edges of the stone bring to mind the crenellation of a fortress. The apartments are set off half a level from one another. Each unit has two entrances and a variety of terraces, and, in some cases, roof terraces. The steel profiles are not encased. Thus, the steel load-bearing members are visible in the apartments, as well.

6
passo
carrabile

N M 1:5000

1961–64

GIÒ PONTI

CHIESA SAN FRANCESCO AL FOPPONINO
MILAN, VIA PAOLO GIOVIO 41

This church is framed by two other buildings belonging to the parish. The facades facing the forecourt are connected by wall segments; the surfaces are unified by cream-toned, faceted tiles. The hexagonal cutouts in the stage-set-like wall segments linking the buildings offer glimpses of the sky. A side entrance to the church [→**192**] is clad in the same faceted tiles. In this design, Ponti explored contrasts: dematerialization versus robustness; thin walls versus volumetric forms; reflective diamond-pointed tiles versus matt, dark brown tiles; windows flush with the facade versus conventional casement windows; and religious motifs versus sleek design. The detailing—for example, the streamlined safety railings—bears witness to Ponti's talent as an industrial designer.

1961–65

VICO MAGISTRETTI

MARINA GRANDE
PINETA DI ARENZANO, PIAZZA DEGLI ULIVI

The Marina Grande complex, located right on the coast of the Mediterranean, connects the beach with Pineta di Arenzano, the weekend colony up on the hill. Magistretti's structure contains residential units, a community center, shops, a garage, and, last but not least, a 350-meter-long platform above a stretch of railroad that once crossed the site. After the railway line was moved inland, this gallery became part of a pedestrian path. Magistretti devised a hybrid building—a cabana megastructure. He incorporated the roof of the railway gallery in the design: it is a terrace high above the beach. To reach the beach you either go down one of the stairs or take the elevator. The bathing huts and cabins are integrated in the concrete structure.

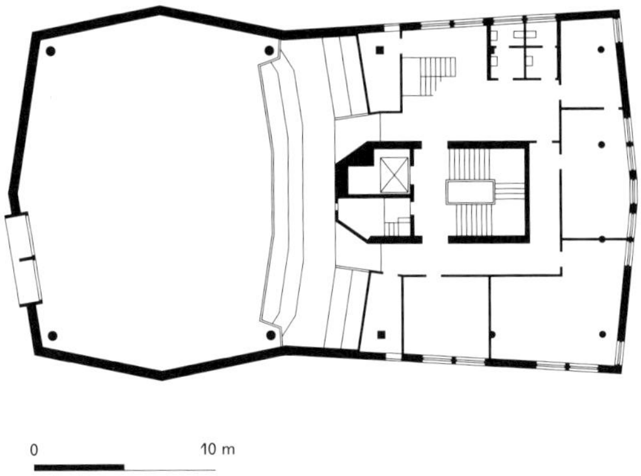

PIERO BOTTONI

CITY HALL

SESTO SAN GIOVANNI, PIAZZA DELLA RESISTENZA

The color concept of the city hall in Sesto San Giovanni, a suburb of Milan, is not easily overlooked. The facade's color gradient ranges from yellow and orange to red, and then to black—as if the lower part had become discolored by water damage or exposure to the elements. But the coloring is deliberate: the effect was achieved with tiles. The entrance level, which has a colonnade on all four sides, is on the second floor. Correspondingly, the square adjoining the city hall is also elevated. On three sides the base supporting the square is bounded by stone walls. On the fourth side [→**201**], it is adjoined by an artificial hill. The main path leading from the street to the entrance ascends its slope.

IL
COMUNE

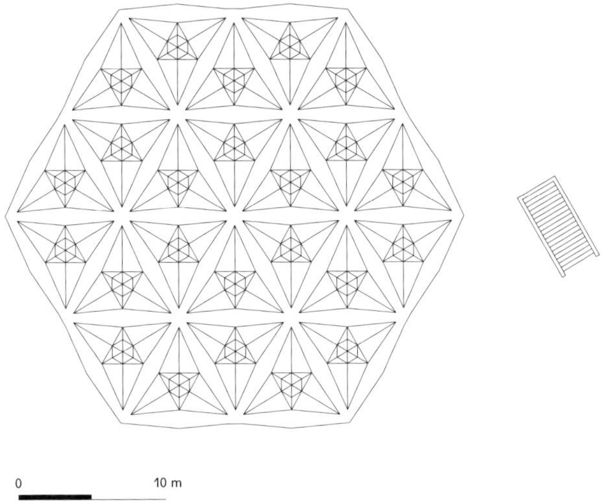

1962–65

FRANCO ALBINI, FRANCA HELG

AMENDOLA SUBWAY STATION
MILAN, PIAZZA GIOVANNI AMENDOLA

Albini & Helg were responsible for the design of twenty-one stations along Milan's Metro Line № 1. With great attention to detail they developed a formal vocabulary that guided the design of the different components, including, for example, the modular wall panels, the distinctive handrails, and the signage. For the station on Piazza Amendola, the duo had the opportunity to devise a roof that brings daylight down to the intermediate level. Their solution is an ornamental roofscape made of translucent fiberglass stars situated within a hexagonal steel frame. The slight peaks and valleys at the edge of the roof retrace the shape of the steel beams, which all have the same profile.

24 ORE
BIGLIETTI
24 ORE
RULLINI FOTOGRAFICI
24 ORE

IGNAZIO GARDELLA

CHIESA SAN NICOLAO DELLA FLUE
MILAN, VIA DALMAZIA 11

The most idiosyncratic—and probably least known—of Gardella'a church designs is dedicated to the Swiss hermit Saint Nicholas of Flüe. The program for this site in a typical neighborhood on the edge of Milan also included a freestanding parsonage and playing fields. The rectangular worship space is raised above the ground. A covered passage runs at ground level along all four sides of the church—inverted cloisters, so to speak. The massing of the church itself cantilevers above it. A monumental outdoor stair in front of the church leads to the elevated entrance. The church is distinguished both inside and out by its striking roof form, which is reminiscent of a curvaceous hat.

1963–66

LUIGI CACCIA DOMINIONI

OFFICE BUILDINGS

MILAN, CORSO EUROPA 11–13

Caccia Dominioni has left his mark on this stretch of the Corso Europa: on one side, with his two office buildings [→**54**], and on the other, with the eclecticist pair of buildings shown here. These tiled structures are connected on the second floor by a bridge; the gesture creates a gateway. While the one on the left makes a unified impression, the one on the right is stratified horizontally. Directly above the bridge, a fully glazed story underscores this layering. Above it are three levels with a balcony at each window and walls clad in tile. The building culminates in another fully glazed story that interlocks with the facade; the glazing is topped by a parapet that doubles as a planter and, last but not least, copper sheeting.

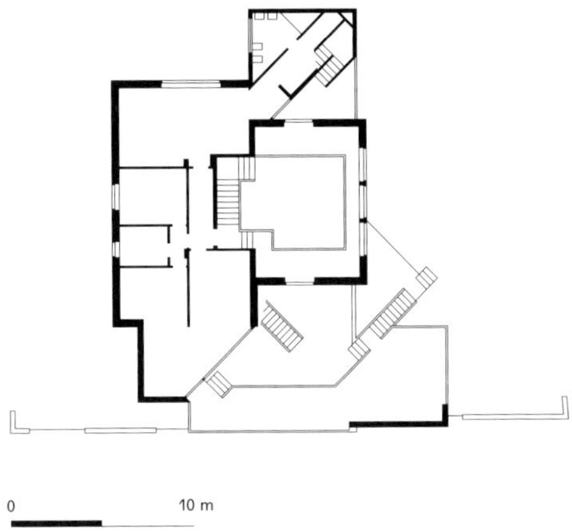

1963–66

GINO VALLE

RESIDENCE

UDINE, VIA TOLMEZZO 74

From the very beginning of Valle's career, his work was marked by a polarity between rationality and technology, on the one hand, and regional construction techniques, on the other. His Zanussi office building [→**134**] is an example of the technological strain. The renovation of this residence in Udine, in contrast, reveals his undogmatic relationship to traditional forms: he extended the roof out past the sidewalk, increased the height of the garden wall, thereby making it part of the house, and unified all exterior surfaces with a coat of stucco. Moreover, he contrasted the building massing's continuous surfaces by making cutouts in surprising locations. For instance, by making incisions in the roof he created idiosyncratic outdoor spaces. Diagonal stairs lead from the garden to the terrace. The path continues to the roof terrace above the double-height living room.

RACCOLTA
VERDE

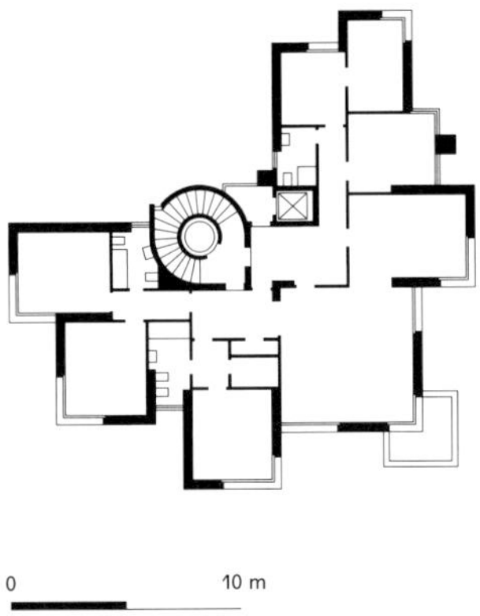

1964–65

VICO MAGISTRETTI

HIGH-RISE APARTMENTS

MILAN, PIAZZALE AQUILEIA, VIA LIPARI

Magistretti designed two residential buildings, each with nine stories, for this corner site: a long slab fronting a square and a slender tower in the garden along Via Lipari. The rooms in the tower are oriented towards the garden and the street. In contrast, the walls closest to the adjacent building have few openings. The balconies positioned at the corners draw attention to the fact that the building is made up of different types of apartments. One type takes up an entire floor. Another type is a duplex, and its living room is a double-height space. Magistretti created sequences of rooms that vary in size; in this way he was able to give the building massing its three-dimensional quality. Like at the Torre al Parco [→ **50**], a separate elevator is linked to the side entrances.

P.le Aquileia

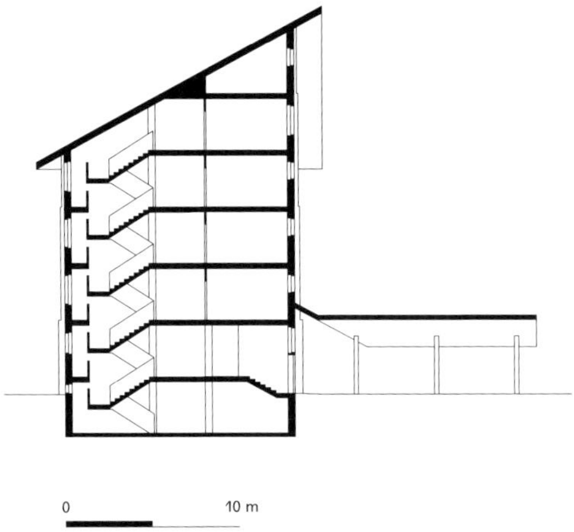

1964–68

ROBERTO GABETTI, AIMARO ISOLA, GIORGIO RAINERI

CASA-ALBERGO ECA
TURIN, VIA DELLE PRIMULE 7

This structure originally served as lodgings and a community center for newly arrived immigrants. At present it is used as a nursing home. It is located in Le Vallette, a neighborhood laid out from 1957 to 1965 on the northwest edge of Turin. Like most of the other buildings here, it has brick exterior walls. So, while the building envelope fits in well with its surroundings, the large roof sets it apart from the other buildings. It seems as if the three architects designed a building double the size and then decided to build only half of it: this would explain why the hip roof is cut down the middle. Two escape stairs were added to the exterior at a later date; they detract from the eccentric, almost surreal impression the building originally made.

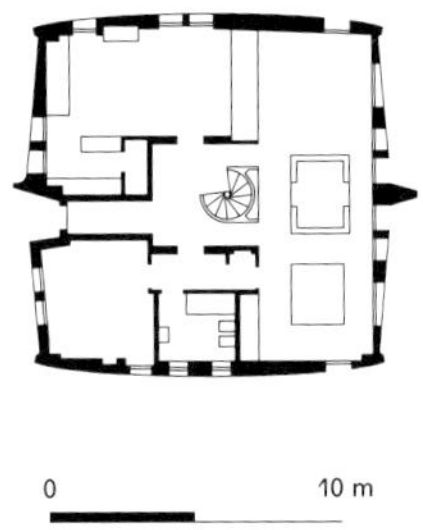

1964–69

GIÒ PONTI, NANDA VIGO

CASA SOTTO UNA FOGLIA
MALO, VIA RAFFAELLO 36

Giò Ponti—founder and, for many years, editor-in-chief of *Domus*—prepared a design of a holiday home nestled "under a leaf." He presented it in issue № 414 of his magazine, provided plans that could be torn out and encouraged his readers to build it. The art collector Giobatta Meneguzzo decided to erect it on a piece of land in Malo—but as a year-round residence capable of holding part of his collection. Because Ponti was unwilling to revise his design, he recommended that the young designer Nanda Vigo make the necessary adaptations. Vigo enlarged the living area by removing the wall between it and the bedroom. The tiled bed stands apart from the walls. She also designed an extravagant "shag" spiral staircase situated at the center of the residence that leads to the art collection on the lower level.

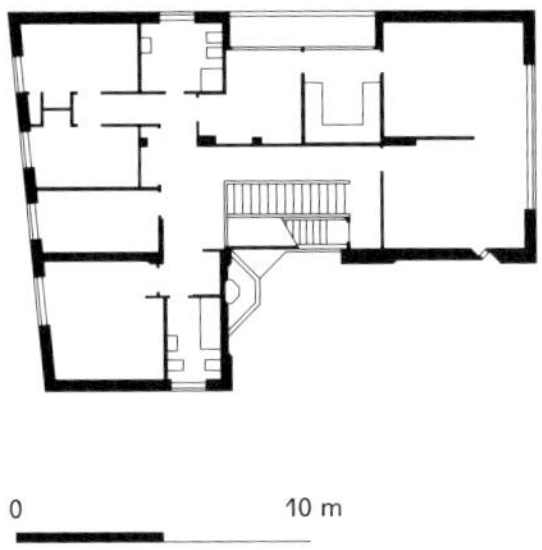

1965–66

GINO VALLE

CASA ROSSA

UDINE, VIA ALESSANDRO VOLTA 24

Casa Rossa is both commonplace and idiosyncratic. Valle sets up connections to traditional architecture and then severs them. This applies, for example, to the overall rectangular form topped with a hip roof and cut open on one side to reveal a staircase and its glazed ceiling. The color of the residence also illustrates this approach: many of the region's buildings are in the same shade of red, but here every single component—including the roof—is coated in it, giving the house its unorthodox look. Subtle moldings and projections structure the facades; the transition from wall to eaves is rounded out. These references to age-old construction techniques are juxtaposed with an unusual detail: Valle made slits in the overhangs. From upper-level interiors, these offer eccentric views of the surroundings.

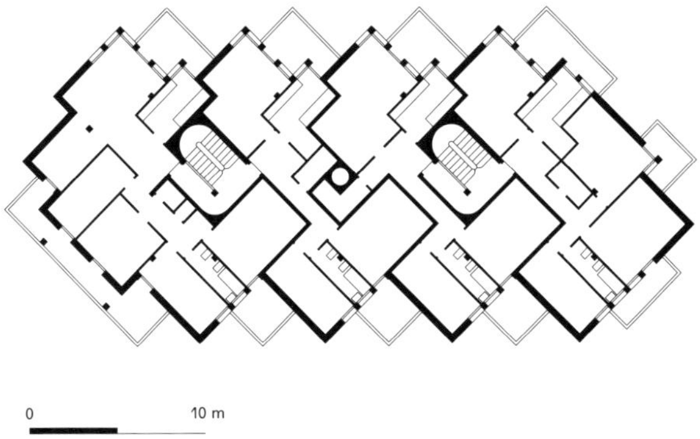

GIUSEPPE GAMBIRASIO

APARTMENT BUILDING
CALOLZIOCORTE, CORSO EUROPA

The building massing of this subsidized apartment block is made up of two identical two-story components—stacked one atop the other. Columns raise the upper two stories and create a remarkable open space on the fourth floor. One doesn't find any signs, however, that the residents use this space. There is one manifestation of the intended use—as noted in the plans—of the space as a playground: the railings on this level are higher than normal. The projections and recessions in the massing give the impression that the building contains two-story units: the apartments do interlock, but each occupies only one level.

1966

MARKET

CALOLZIOCORTE
municipio
polizia municipale
carabinieri
COMO
LECCO
MILANO
BERGAMO
CAPRINO B.
CISANO B.
MONTE MARENZO
TORRE DE BUSI
VALCAVA
CARENNO
STOP

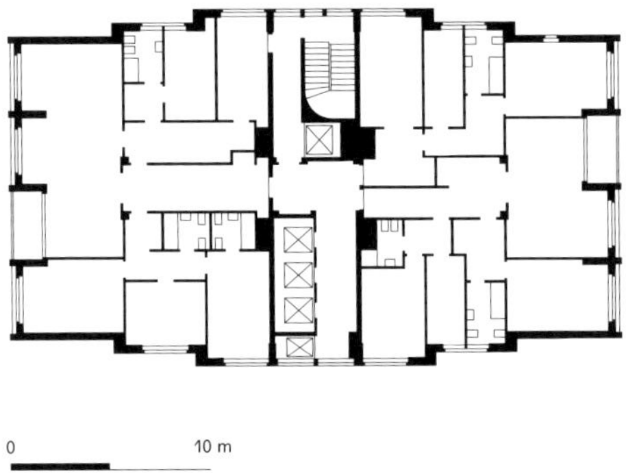

1966–69

GIOVANNI MUZIO

TORRE TURATI

MILAN, PIAZZA DELLA REPUBBLICA, VIA FILIPPO TURATI 40

The neighborhood surrounding Torre Turati offers a rare opportunity to see three major works by an architect who for decades steadily developed his architectural vocabulary: the Ca'Brütta (1919–22), which is a manifesto of the *Novecento Milanese* movement; the eleven-story apartment block on Piazza della Repubblica (1935–36), a massive, stately assembly of bricks; and finally, the Torre Turati itself, Muzio's most noteworthy late-modernist design. The slender tower's steel structure is clad in prefabricated concrete panels. The ground floor is dedicated to shops. Offices occupy the stories above the ground floor. The levels that project out beyond the base contain apartments.

IP

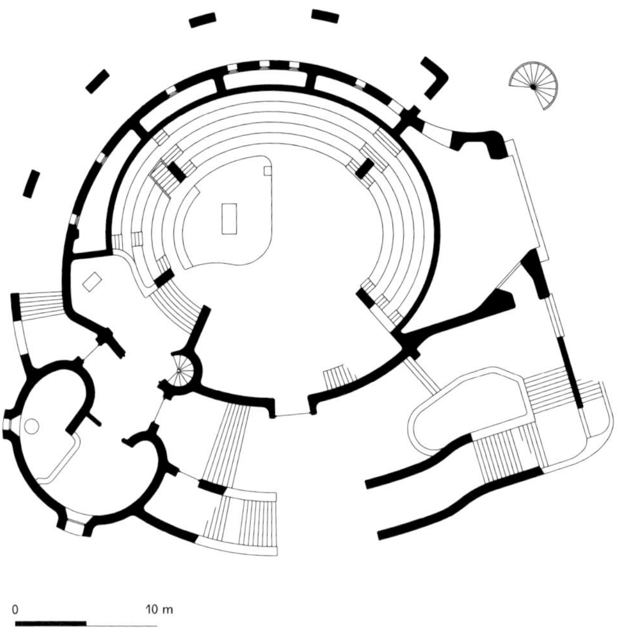

GIOVANNI MICHELUCCI

CHIESA DELL'IMMACOLATA CONCEZIONE DI MARIA VERGINE
LONGARONE, VIA ROMA, PIAZZA JACOPO TASSO

1966–78

This church is a memorial to the Vajont dam disaster. In 1963, a landslide sent the soil, rubble and vegetation of nearly an entire mountainside into the reservoir, causing water to pour over the dam and flood the town of Longarone. Nearly 2000 people perished, and almost all of the buildings were washed away. Michelucci's design for the new church stacks two elliptical amphitheaters atop one another: the one on ground level is an enclosed space with indirect lighting and oblique walls, and the one above it, an open-air fellowship space with a view of the ill-fated valley. On the church's perimeter, a broad ascent combining ramps and stairs spirals up to the roofscape. This part of the building in particular draws attention to the complexity of the exposed-concrete building, as well as to the artistry of the carpenters who built the formwork.

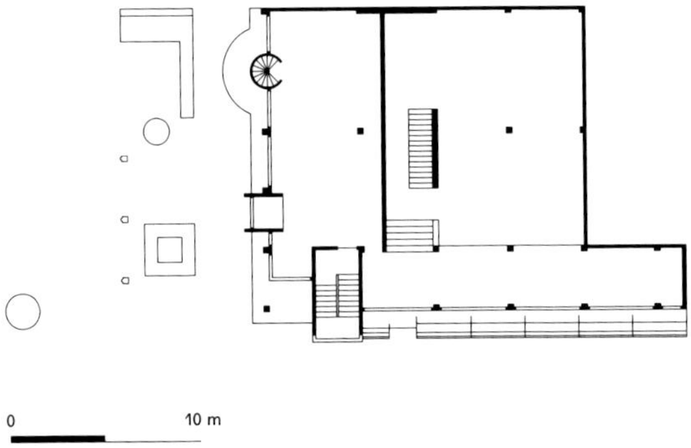

IGINIO CAPPAI, PIETRO MAINARDIS

CASA GIALLA

MIRA, VIA ANTONIO GRAMSCI 13

1967–69

In 1967, the architects began work on the Olivetti Hotel [→**262**] and this mixed-use building. In comparison to the hotel, Casa Gialla almost seems simple: it consists of low-slung building massing with a pitched roof. The facade facing the small square is organized by means of engaged columns. The street facade, in contrast, is machine-like: the architects themselves considered it a "combine harvester" parked on the street in a small town. The curved mesh screening the windows rolls up at the push of a button. The gateway at the main entrance slides to the side. The unifying deep yellow makes the building appear to be a vision of the future. At the time of construction, yellow had been deemed the color of the year 2000.

SA GIALLA

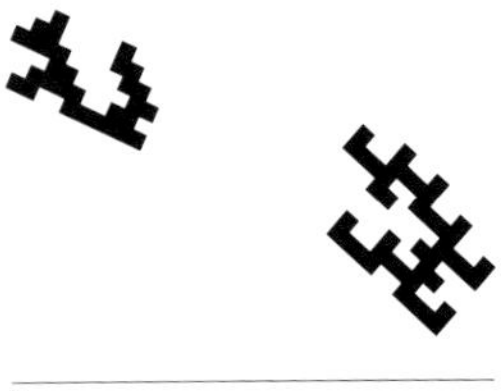

M 1:5000

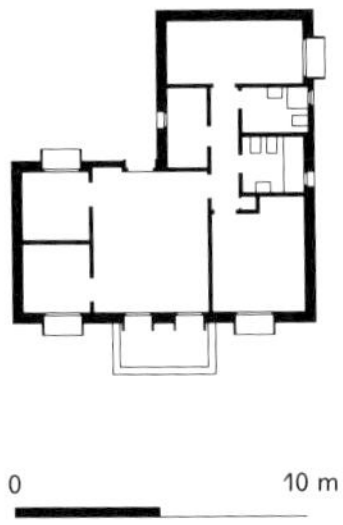

1967–70

VICO MAGISTRETTI

HOLIDAY HOMES

FRAMURA, LOCALITÀ VANDARECCA

These holiday homes were inserted with great care in a seaside cliff. Arranged in two groups, they literally cling to the mountainside. The project shows that the architecture of leisure can be sensitive to its surroundings—in contrast to the rampant resort and hotel development that began to take over entire stretches of the coastline in the late nineteen-sixties. It also exemplifies Magistretti's attempt to find a balance between rationalism and local building traditions. The impression the domiciles make depends on the viewer's standpoint: from the street their massing and color—a familiar dark red—recall anonymous architecture, while from above, attention is directed to the intricacies of the roofscape and the distribution of the massing around courtyards. Seen from the beach, the cluster of units closer to the sea forms a unified block.

masters; Persico, who died in 1936, was a critic of European standing. In Austria during these years there were no comparable voices anymore; thanks to his wife Carmela Prati de Vitorelli—who was employed as costume designer at the Scala in Milan—starting in the late twenties, Oswald Haerdtl (who first worked for Josef Hoffmann and later became his partner) was familiar with Milan's newest trends. In 1930, he was responsible for Austria's contribution to the Triennale in Monza and was also represented later at the 5th Triennale in Milan and remained in contact with Giò Ponti.

Haerdtl's works, as well as buildings and interiors by Josef Frank & Oskar Wlach, were presented in *Domus*, the magazine Ponti founded in 1928; in 1948/49, Haerdtl studied Milan's newest buildings and interiors in situ and imported the so-called "espresso style" to Vienna, though on account of its decorative aspects it was not really held in high regard by his colleagues here. Nevertheless, it has to this day left behind traces of a distinct attitude towards life in the urban milieu. Following her husband's death, Carmela Prati-Haerdtl, who was related to Ponti's wife, served for decades as Vienna's *Domus* correspondent.

In 1936, Giò Ponti renovated the Italian Cultural Institute in Vienna's third district and it was through him that a second, probably even more interesting axis of trans-Alpine exchange transpired: in 1932, Bernard Rudofsky left Vienna for southern Italy. There he worked with Luigi Cosenza on large competitions and buildings, and in 1936/37 he and Cosenza realized the Dr. Oro Residence in Posilippo/Naples, which was promptly prominently published in *Casabella* and *Architectural Review*. In 1937, he went to Milan to work with Giò Ponti and with him developed a large hotel on Capri and

an injudicious policy and an unbearable situation of deterioration. The reply of the government, at that time a stable coalition of the Christian Democratic and Socialist parties, was the adoption of a new planning and housing law in 1967. It required the communes at long last to equip themselves with regulative plans and prescribed urbanistic standards, thus offering a remedy, however weak, for one of the fundamental deficiencies in Italian legislations. The impact of these measures, however, has proved to be marginal with respect to the ever greater changes in the national political picture.

OLAF MÖLLER: "PIER PAOLO PASOLINI AND ITALIAN CINEMA IN THE 1960S," IN: *PROGRAM OF THE AUSTRIAN FILM MUSEUM* № 1/2009, VIENNA 2009, P. 3
In the 1960s, Italian cinema reached the pinnacle of both its artistic splendour and international influence. Masters of worldwide stature such as Michelangelo Antonioni, Federico Fellini, Luchino Visconti, and, some time later, Bernardo Bertolucci, set new standards for *auteur* filmmaking, while the Italian film industry had become Europe's

the following year was also editor of several editions of Domus, where his seminal essays, cultural views, as well as drawings and projects were presented for the first time in concentrated form. During these years, the influence of Frank & Wlach and especially of Rudofsky on Ponti was extraordinary, as is revealed in Ponti's dictum: "The Mediterranean taught Rudofsky, and Rudofsky taught me."

I'll skip a bit and, at the end of this second-to-last fragmentary note, make reference to the first international publications on Hoffmann and Loos that appeared in Italy after the war: in 1956, a book by Giulia Veronesi on Hoffmann and the one by Ludwig Münz on Loos by the Milanese publisher *Il Balcone*; in 1959, *Casabella* dedicated an entire issue to Adolf Loos, with essays by Rogers and Rossi. Moreover: Manfredo Tafuri presented the first critical-analytical publication of international standing on the architecture of social-democratic Vienna in 1980—*Vienna Rossa*, at Electa. (I recall a scene in Café Sperl in which Tafuri, who both had an impressive physiognomy and the professorial and worldly bearing of Umberto Eco, appeared with his local "scout" Wolfgang Podgorschek, who helped him prepare excursions and visits to archives.)

And vice versa: important texts by and on Aldo Rossi, by Giorgio Grassi (disturbingly up to date!), by Daniele Vitale on Giuseppe Terragni, on the gripping clashes between *Novecentisti*, rationalists and modernists in the Italy of the late nineteen-thirties first appeared in Vienna around 1980 in the first issue of the magazine *UMBAU*—founded by the *Österreichische Gesellschaft für Architektur* (*ÖGFA*) and dedicated to architecture, reflection, and theory.

film centre ... In contrast to almost all other important filmmaking nations of the 1960s, Italian cinema experienced no radical break with established structures. The backbone of Italian film culture, which was based on Neorealism, enjoyed so much consensus that it seemed able to support any extreme positions and aesthetic developments whatsoever. Iconoclasts such as Marco Bellocchio (*I pugni in tasca / Fists in the Pocket*) and Marco Ferreri (*Dillinger è morto / Dillinger is Dead*) could develop their talents with close ties to the industry ...

MARTIN ROSEFELDT, IN: *ARTE DVD-NEWS*, 25/10/06, WWW.ARTE-TV
"The Red Desert"—that's what Antonioni named the rusting and toxic industrial landscape around Ravenna (Emilia Romana) presented to the viewer from the very first frame onward ... In his first color movie, instead of simply filming the colors as encountered, Antonioni immediately submitted his new means of expression to strict compositional principles. Amid a backdrop of pervasive shades of gray and brown,

THIRTEENTH NOTE

I'll try to return to the motif, to the message of this collection of photos by taking a look at four enigmatic images.

Here [→223] we have a house with a pitched roof, substantial roof projections, small windows, fine bas-relief in the facade. It is a rather common building type, but on one corner, plainly pulled apart and at the same time, as whole, with rust red hue, tied together again visually, and namely with a colorful skin that uniformly coats everything, alienates, related to the region's traditional house colors and yet different: simultaneously day-to-day and artificial; amid the ever-present red, the green of the lush trees and shrubs surrounding the house seems even more intense, almost artificial; *Casa Rossa*, an early work by the great Gino Valle previously unknown to me ...

Another photo [→241], another color dominates: *Casa Gialla*—an architecture in high relief, shifting between neo-plasticity and machine aesthetics, like the body of a gleaming car coated in an all-encompassing bright yellow layer of lacquer. With a level of detail and color intensity that neatly carries over to the ground, continues on and expands in the forecourt, transforms into the built landscape and, on account of the architecture's *compulsion* to design, subtly yet relentlessly "envelops," domesticates and presents the venerable olive tree ...

The third [→199]: a Tachist color gradient cloaking the building from deep black below to bright red on the main part to yellowish orange below the roof, clearly made of mosaic or small, multi-colored tiles, on top of that, five different window formats close together—and an undulating hem above

he had the pipes painted bright blue and red, plants blackened or sometimes even dipped in a toxic shade of purple, surrounded by reddish-orange rusting tanks and a disoriented heroine—Monica Vitti—dressed in toxic green. Antonioni paints his movie like a canvas; through the sparingly employed colors he creates a certain mood as a commentary—conceived as a substitute for music—directed to the viewers. Over the course of the movie, this highly stylized commentary, complemented by sparingly employed music, has an increasingly strong effect, for example, when Monica Vitti, following a stay at a hospital and in search of a purpose in life, wants to open a boutique in the middle of a bleak, gray street (in which even the display of a peddler's cart is drab); she is looking for the right color for her shop, but doesn't find it.

the arcade, and the "nature" inhabiting the forecourt, in turn, is celebrated and subdued in a ceramic, styled "dog bowl" ...

As a final image [→256], a well-known residential complex in the neo-rationalism of the nineteen-seventies: unmistakable, volumetric pathos of building massing reduced to primary shapes, yet here too both the geometry's rigor and the metaphysical melancholy that characterized the projects by Aldo Rossi and by Carlo Aymonino are upended in unexpected dimensions by the interplay of colors.

The drawings and images we had seen of the Gallaratese district were mostly black-and-white; with these colors, above all with the continuous, red-toned concrete floor, the seemingly mute architecture—scaled back to an armature of all of the meanings and aspirations in changing sunlight, with its shadows and reflections—takes on a subliminal, vibrating sensuousness.

If contemplated with curiosity, patience, and open eyes, it becomes clear that all of these images address similar aesthetic questions and can draw us into an unending labyrinth of possible messages and realities. Let's recall the maxims of neorealism and the visual effects of Pop Art, the ideas of *Radical Design*, of *Alchimia,* and *Memphis*: design of buildings and products seeking to come very close to day-to-day life, to not impose an artificial, visionary aesthetic on it *top down*, but rather to further develop, *bottom up*, the qualities of the self-evident. But there is, of course, no longer anything self-evident in modern capitalist consumer culture.

The neorealism of the postwar years was followed in quick succession by the technoid phase of the boom years—obsessed with progress and glamour—accompanying which, equally as quickly an alternative parallel

TAFURI, DAL CO: OP. CIT., PP. 387–390
Only in the work of the Italian Aldo Rossi (b. 1931) do we encounter the programmatic search for the place where form can regain the use of the architect's language. Rossi has one thing in common with Kahn: the insistence on giving concrete shape to nostalgia. His architecture certifies the decease of all logical order in the architectural discourse and the affirmation of the bourgeois universe. Yet what he expresses is not regret for the absence of a happier world before that changeover but, rather, a nostalgia for a language from an even earlier world. Like Kahn, Rossi struggles to conjure away the loss of the center, but he places no hope in any help from outside. For him, logic can affirm itself only to the extent that the language is born out of a continually varied aggregation of a few words restored to their original semantic value ... Such a quest for a way of communicating that would not lose the patrimony of personal and collective memories makes the apparent simplicity of Rossi decidedly complex.

world of anti-consumerism opened up, or better yet: the postulate of the self-determined individualist, the anti-technocratic unshackling of the libido. The *Radical Design* project, which had already gotten its start in the nineteen-sixties, and *Arte povera* again tried to take the neorealist path, but with other means and a demystified consciousness. It was an attempt to escape the consumerist fashion cycles, the rotation of the capitalist consumer world around its own axis, in such a way that one incorporates its "feigned" aesthetic postulations again in the "actual" trivial forces of cultural patterns and desires and thereby revise the alienation, the unauthenticity of the only seemingly "right life in the wrong one."

The Italian designers and architects of this era attempted to "culturize the banal," to activate what had been stigmatized by the upper class and the elitist canon as kitsch in all of its highly complex dimensions; on the other hand, they attempted to re-mythicize and re-poeticize technologies accelerated to the point of immateriality, to once again make visible the elementary magic of the simplest, most natural, humane, "unmediated" values and realities.

These photos, with the specific vantage point and synthetic selection, show us that northern Italy—like no other region—experienced and reflected upon the dynamic upheavals of postwar Europe and the boom years, these industrial-cultural accelerations, on the one hand, and the movements resisting middle-class conformism, on the other, in the film, literature, design, and architecture it produced—with personalities like Pasolini and Ponti, Rossi and Sottsass, Antonioni, Rogers, Eco, Fellini, Pistoletto, Visconti, Berlinguer, Bertolucci, Calvino, etc., whose poetic

VOLKER FISCHER: *DESIGN NOW. INDUSTRY OR ART?*, MUNICH 1989, PP. 73–74
The "Radical Design" movement began in Italy back in the mid-sixties. It was opposed to the classic Italian postwar style of "Bel Disegno" then prevailing, which was associated with such designers as Giò Ponti, Marco Albini, Vico Magistretti, Mario Bellini, the Castiglionis, Joe Colombo, Marco Zanuso, Afra and Tobia Scarpa, Gae Aulenti, Gianfranco Frattini, etc. The Radical Design groups such as Superstudio, Archizoom, Zziggurat and Studio 45, and later also their manufacturing association, Global Tools, projected the popular aesthetic of Pop Art onto the design scene. If misgivings about a consumer society that inflated both production and consumption to self-destructive levels could logically be expressed at all in the design of products, then only in those which rebel against unthinking production and consumption. Certainly the most far-reaching protest against the dogmas of functionalism and "good taste" in design sprouted from ground prepared by Radical Design and began with the foundation of Studio Alchimia in Milan in 1978/79 ... The chief publicist for the group was and is Mendini, who from

resistance to the "superstitions of progress" of every ideology, against the normativity of the industrial complex in its smallest orbit, is condensed in extraordinary fashion, in their biographies, works and deeds.

Furthermore, this album shows us that the claim to synthesization—the rebuttal of normatively treated opposites, the passionate contamination and reassessment of the cultural codes in the undogmatic "gusto"—did not first have an effect during postmodernism, but was already active in the early fifties, as, for example, Caccia Dominioni's oeuvre demonstrates, which back then came into existence below the sensitivity threshold of the professional media and that, almost logically, in turn, was first adequately reviewed—and made accessible for contemporary positions and inquiries—in the nineteen-nineties by young architects in Switzerland.

What inspiration might such photos of our most recent architectural history give—not just in Italy, but especially flagrant there—a time and a discipline that has again clearly become more restricted, more pragmatic, and lacking in perspective? What might that be? A timeless message shines through these images—recorded from the perspective of "dilettantes"—of long-ago-completed buildings: Eros, who, as Ponti said of Rudofsky, has been lent wings by the Mediterranean, yet possesses a universally valid attitude toward life, toward building, toward individuality, and toward the undeterred quest for a balance between a wholly tangible, necessary usefulness and an every-bit-as-necessary inspiring uselessness—which is so much more difficult to grasp, understand, reason, tolerate, and place.

1960 onwards was editor of *Casabella* and *Modo* and then publisher of *Domus*. Sottsass left Alchimia in 1981 when Memphis was founded … Sottsass propagates a non-culture which is unspecific in social and hierarchical terms, and thus belongs to no one and, at the same time, to everyone. He celebrates the iconography of the commonplace, which in this case is also fed by his experience of and affinity with the unabashed banality of design in the cultures of many non-European peoples …

GIORGIO GRASSI: "FORMALISM IN MODERN ARCHITECTURE," IN: *UMBAU* 4, VIENNA 1981, P. 6

(From a lecture held at Berlin's *Akademie der Künste* in February 1974)

It appears that it is nearly impossible for contemporary architecture to steer clear of the magic of experimentalism per se, the magic of "new form." To steer clear of something—which is in fact a true "superstition of the new." I repeat: this is above all a problem of content, of values, because the very cultural framework of capitalism is extraordinarily formalistic. But that doesn't mean that "taking a stand against it" necessarily has to occur on its own territory. On the contrary.

GIANNI PETTENA IN A LECTURE AT THE *ARCHITEKTURZENTRUM WIEN*, VIENNA, 25 NOVEMBER 2009
You can see our research and performances in the sixties and early seventies as a time of practising architecture through the tools of art ... and this was also very much stimulated and characterised by the joy of refusing the culture of the fathers.

ASTRID STAUFER: "BEYOND THE DEBATE. ON THE CRITICAL RECEPTION OF THE WORK OF LUIGI CACCIA DOMINIONI," IN: *STAUFER & HASLER ARCHITEKTEN / ARCHITECTS. THESEN / THESES*, SULGEN / ZURICH 2009, P. 65
From today's point of view the buildings by the Milanese architect Luigi Caccia Dominioni appear to be near-exemplary works of what has been referred to as "contextual building" and "thematisation of conditions" since Aldo Rossi began exercising his influence on the Swiss architectural scene. Already from the late 1940s onwards, each of Caccia Dominioni's results is tailored to the location and brief of the construction project. Conversely, each result projects a striking, highly charged image that, quite surprisingly, leads the observer straight back to its origins ... As in the Chase Manhattan Bank on Piazza Meda, for example, Caccia had often been subtly criticized for his ingratiating, and above all "unpedagogical," combination of buildings from various eras. It wasn't until the onset of the new millennium that his approach began to be appreciated as a positive contribution—which in the current architectural culture of Switzerland is referred to as "Weiterbauen," i.e., "building on," and considered an almost general prerequisite.

OTTO KAPFINGER
*1949, lives in Vienna. Works as publicist, critic, exhibition curator, lecturer, and juror. Studied architecture from 1967 to 1972 at the Technical University of Vienna. First trip to Italy in the summer of 1968: Venice, Florence, Rome, Naples, Salerno. In 1970, with Angela Hareiter and Adolf Krischanitz, founding of *Missing Link*; until 1978 (Hareiter until 1974) collective transdisciplinary theoretical and artistic-practical projects in the areas performance art, conceptual art, streetwork, painting, and experimental film.

From 1970 to 1976: solo shows, participation in group shows, multi-media presentations: Trigon in Graz, Impact Gallery in Lausanne, Museum of the Twentieth Century Vienna, ADI Milan, Summer Session of the International Institute of Design in London, Palazzoli Gallery in Milan, *Neue Galerie* at the *Landesmuseum Joanneum* (now *Universalmuseum Joanneum*) in Graz, *Künstlerhaus* in Salzburg, *Schlossberg Art Fair* in Graz, *Music Forum* in Breitenbrunn, *Österreichische Gesellschaft für Architektur* in Vienna, *Supersommer* in Vienna. Publications about *Missing Link* appeared in *Casabella—rivista di urbanistica architettura e disegno industriale*, Milan, № 392–393/1974, pp. 58–60 and № 411/1976, pp. 14–24.

Notes 1–13 documents the diary-like notations Kapfinger made from July 12 to 26, 2011. During the same period of time, the excerpts reproduced for this volume—which accompany, annotate, complement, deepen and contradict the notes, in most cases synchronously, but sometimes deliberately asynchronously—emerged from the accompanying research.

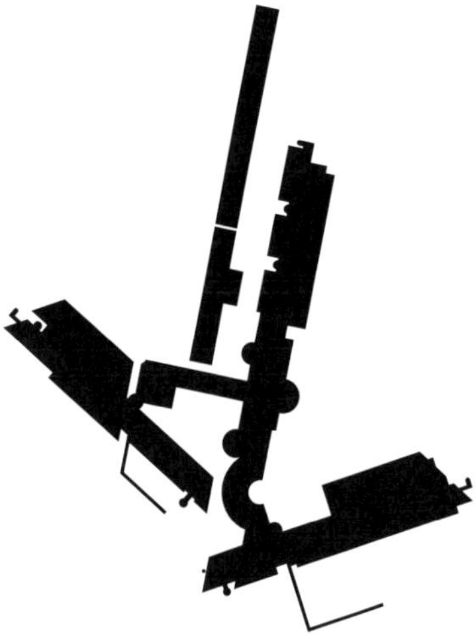

N M 1:5000

1967–74

CARLO AYMONINO, ALDO ROSSI

GALLARATESE HOUSING COMPLEX
MILAN, VIA CILEA 34, VIA FALCK 37

Aymonino and Rossi both taught in Venice. The housing complex they designed together reveals two contrasting notions of architecture. Aymonino, from Rome, had a background in neorealism. For this complex, he developed a wide range of apartment types; in combination with a circulation concept rich in variety he achieved extraordinary plasticity and complexity. Rossi, from Milan, had a background in journalism. He sought reduction in his design and contraposed Aymonino's reddish-brown, expressive building massing with an ascetic white block. Rossi's design makes reference to autonomous, fundamental forms and typologies. The result is rigorous: the ground floor is an open hall delineated by piers and columns. Both architects were interested in producing paths and squares—but in this project they are not accessible to the public.

75 m

0
10 m

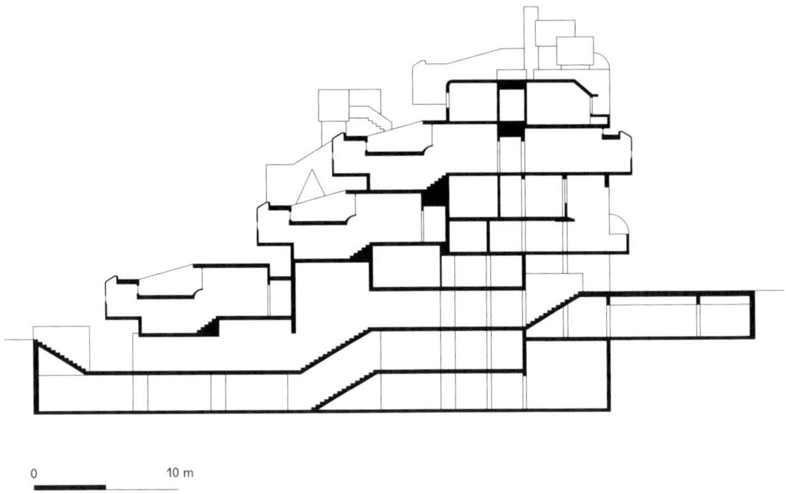

1967–75

IGINIO CAPPAI, PIETRO MAINARDIS

OLIVETTI HOTEL

IVREA, CORSO BOTTA 30

This structure commissioned by Olivetti brings to mind a giant typewriter. It is one of the rare examples in which a radical project developed in the nineteen-sixties did not remain on paper. The building contains apartments, conference rooms, a restaurant, a bar, and a swimming pool. Olivetti planned to use it as a training center for employees from around the world. After a short time, however, it was converted into a hotel. The individual capsules are conceived of as compact houses: each has its own living area and kitchen, a cockpit-like study with sliding roof, a sunken sleeping area with adjoining bathroom, and a roof terrace. Like the berth of a boat, these spaces are all arranged in a highly compact fashion.

HOTEL LA SERRA
INEMA
ABC
ABCinema d'essai
AUDITORIUM LA SERRA
INGRESSO
Break House

PASSO
CARRABILE

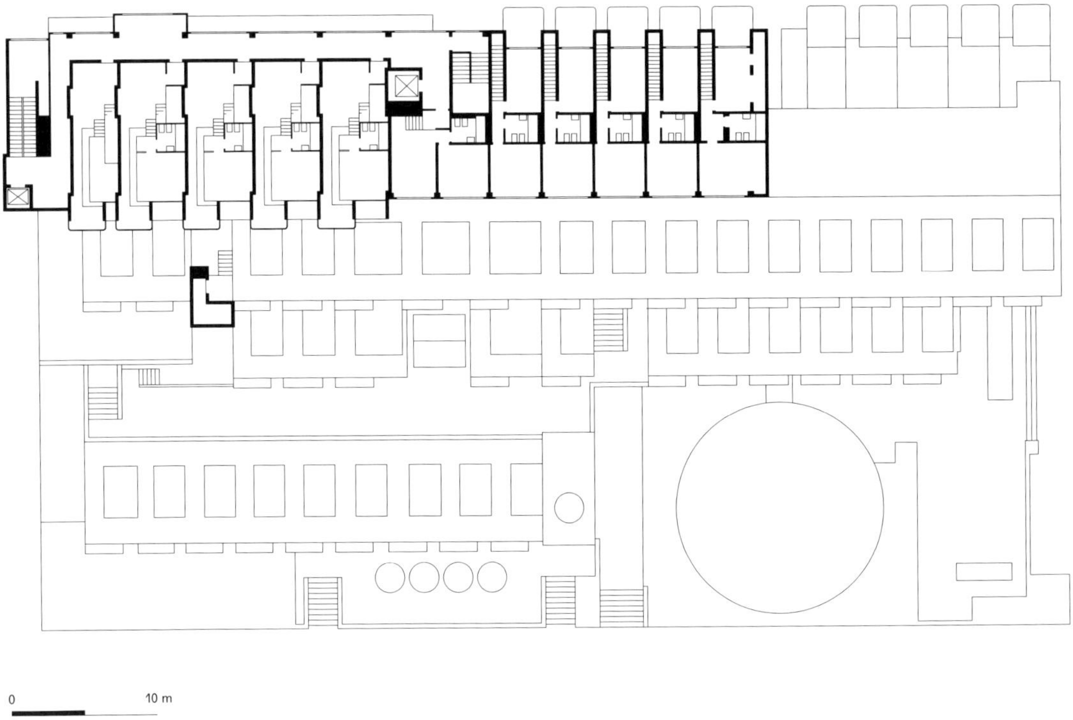

0
10 m

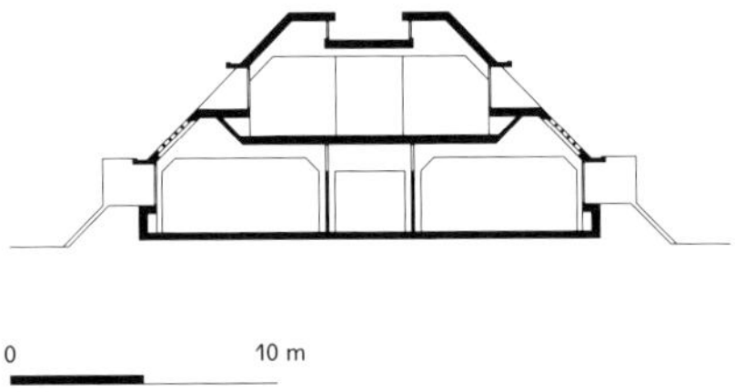

1968–70

IGINIO CAPPAI, PIETRO MAINARDIS

SCHOOL

MIRA, ORIAGO, VIA LAGO DI LECCO

The school building—located in a flat landscape amid single-family houses and sports fields—resembles a berm. Both the form of its building massing and the entrance concept are unconventional. In addition to the main entrance there is a series of secondary entrances—one of them is even on the roof. A stair integrated in the roof provides access both to the roof terrace and to a secondary entrance on the upper level—in other words, it is also possible to enter the school via this detour. To fulfill the school authority's requirements, Cappai and Mainardis had to include conventional central corridors. But they also saw to it that the classrooms on the ground floor are accessible directly from the exterior: each of them has a cube-shaped appendage and its own entrance.

N M 1:5000

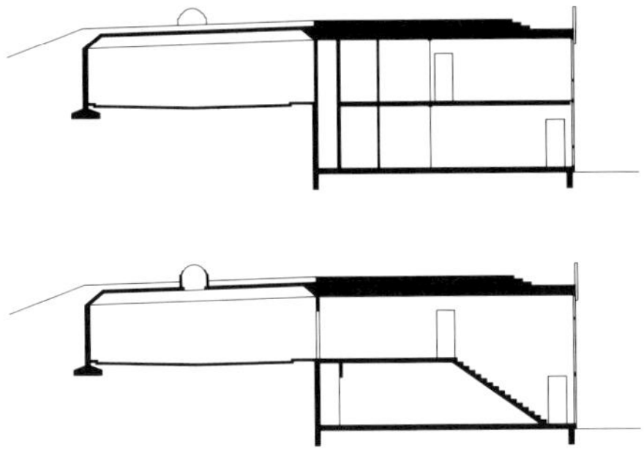

0 10 m

1968–74

ROBERTO GABETTI, AIMARO ISOLA

OLIVETTI APARTMENT BUILDING
IVREA, VIA CARANDINI 6

With this project, Olivetti once again made an extraordinary conceptual experiment possible: in this case, the company commissioned an apartment building for its employees. The units are partially underground, and in some respects the structure looks more like land art than a building. Ivreans refer to it—not without reason—as *Talponia* (molehill). From the outer perimeter only a berm is visible. Its roof is a broad, surreal promenade—but is not connected to any other networks of paths. Not until you enter the enigmatic berm does it become clear that it holds a building. Sheathed in a delicate glass skin, eighty efficiency units and twelve two-story units are arranged around a sunken courtyard with a diameter of 137.5 meters. Embedded within the berm, a street with adjacent parking provides access to the apartments.

GIOVANNI MICHELUCCI

PARSONAGE

ARZIGNANO, VIA MONTE GRAPPA, VIA LOBBIE

This parsonage is part of a complex that also includes the church San Giovanni Battista and a primary school. All three buildings were planned by Michelucci, but they vary in design. In contrast to the three-dimensionality of his nineteen-sixties church designs, for the parsonage he employs a system of "building blocks" and steel profiles. His creation is akin to a covered market square in which the required spaces are suspended from or placed within the framework. The project gives the impression that it was intended to be readily adaptable, but the design is in fact fully resolved: the spaces inserted within the framework have brick walls, a sign of permanence. The open space at the rear containing a stair and a gallery is at once a loggia and a stage.

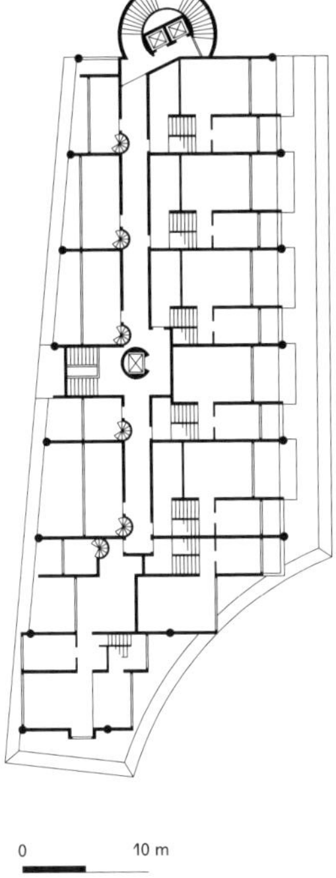

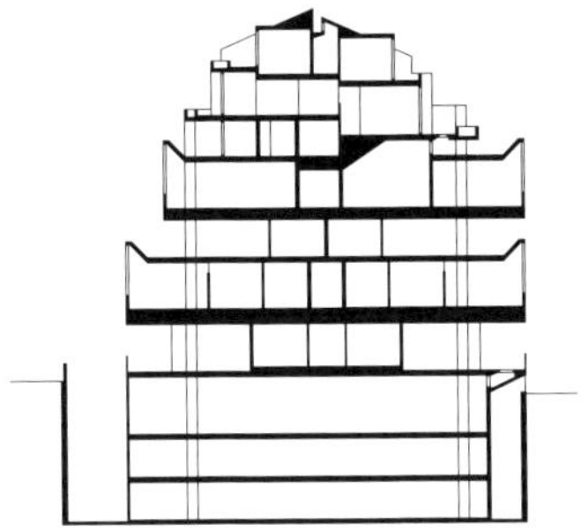

1969–71

WALTER BARBERO, GIUSEPPE GAMBIRASIO, GIORGIO ZENONI

MIXED-USE BUILDING

BERGAMO, ROTONDA DEI MILLE, VIA PICCININI

Both formally and functionally, this is a hybrid building. The multiple programs it accommodates are expressed in the design of the different levels: the impression is of separate layers. The cinema, the garage and storage spaces are located in the three underground stories. On the ground floor are the shops and passageways, and on the second and fourth floors, the offices. On the third floor, a parking deck interrupts the building massing. Topping off the building is a zone that extends three stories. It contains twelve multi-level apartments and terraces: the treatment of the massing yields a differentiated roofscape and reaches its culmination at the side of the building facing a circular piazza, the Rotonda dei Mille. The two office levels retrace the piazza's shape, but are not aligned: the centers of the circles are slightly shifted.

1969–72

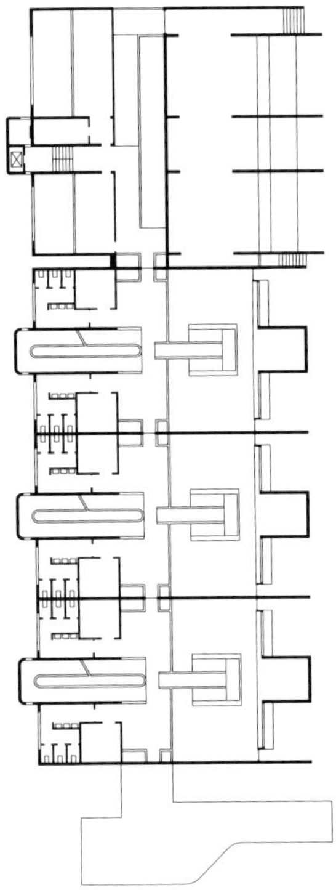

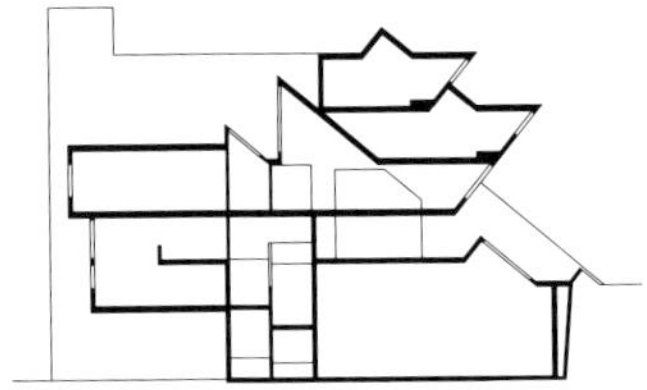

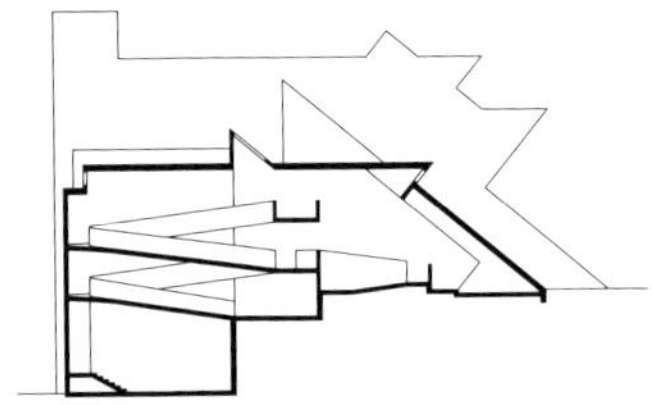

0 10 m

BARAN CIAGÀ, GIUSEPPE GAMBIRASIO

PRESCHOOL

BERGAMO, CURNO, VIA ABRUZZI

This preschool has a classroom wing with six classes, an underground gym, and a commons containing the administration spaces, a cafeteria, and staff flats. The architects designed a depictive building whose oblique walls continue to the ground. All structural walls and roof surfaces are made of reinforced concrete. The oblique wall and roof surfaces were originally coated in colorful, textured layers of fiberglass. This coating is both a sealing layer and a component of the design. Parts of it are intact. Still more unusual than the building's form is its circulation concept, which consists of internal paths, ramps, and balconies. The low-ceilinged corridor running the length of the building contrasts starkly with the three lofty sets of ramps perpendicular to it.

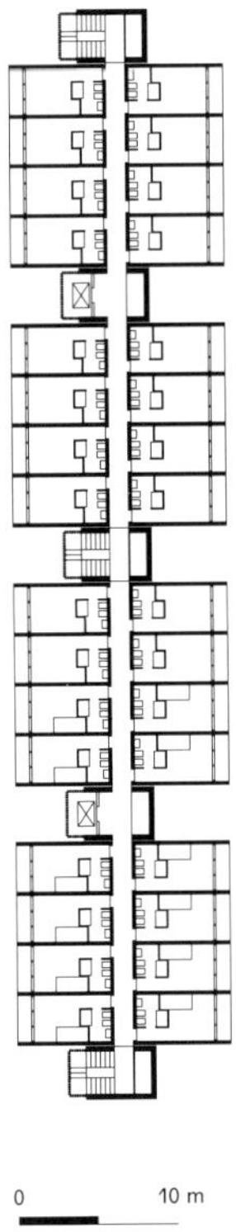

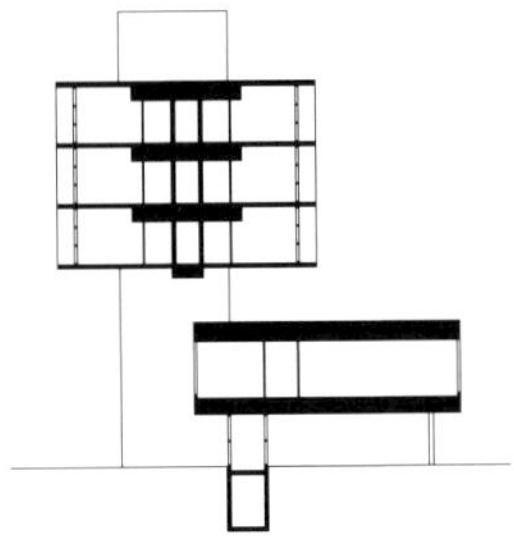

1970–74

BRUNO MORASSUTTI

IBM TRAINING CENTER

NOVEDRATE, VIA EUROPA UNITA, VIA DELLA COSTA

IBM's training center looks like a cross between corporate architecture and a university campus. It is a world of its own, with playing fields and other recreational facilities. Morassutti grouped the auditoria and laboratories, the administration, and the cafeteria in buildings that stay close to the ground. For the residential buildings he developed an unconventional concept in which cubes are suspended from reinforced concrete piers. A unit consists of twenty-four single rooms, each with its own bathroom. There are ten such room groups in total, plus two additional groups with living spaces for the teaching staff. The suspension structure is in steel. The concrete piers alternately contain an elevator or a staircase. After IBM moved out, with a small number of adaptations the complex was transformed into a university campus.

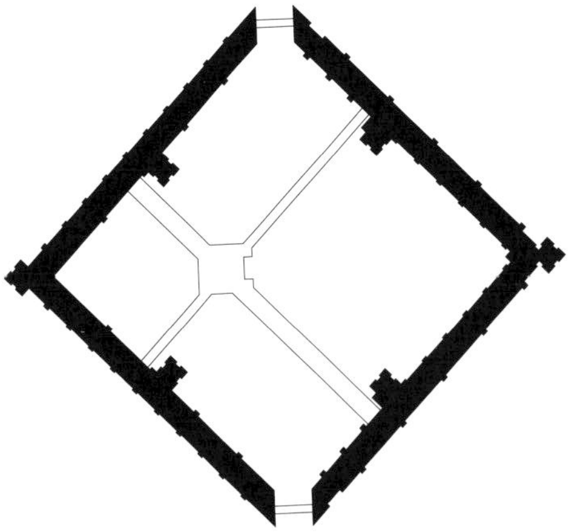

N M 1:5000

1970–83

CARLO CELLI, LUCIANO CELLI, DARIO TOGNON

ROZZOL MELARA HOUSING COMPLEX
TRIESTE, VIA PASTEUR

This megastructure containing subsidized flats was planned by twenty-nine local firms under the direction of Celli & Tognon. The steep topography was left largely intact. Consequently, there is no ground floor, and in both structures the entrance levels are situated high above the ground. The entrance level serves as the main component of the circulation concept. Stairs and lifts lead from this promenade with shops and community rooms to the apartments. The upper structure's circulation level is part of a circuit; the two structures are linked via bridges extending from this level to the roof of the lower structure. In an extension of the circulation level of the lower structure, covered pathways crisscross the courtyard [→**296**]. Forty staircases intersect with the two circulation levels; each stair provides access to two apartments per level.

M 1:5000

1971

ANGELO MANGIAROTTI

HOLIDAY HOMES
COSTERMANO, VILLAGGIO PARCO MURLONGO

In his design, Mangiarotti freely distributed a variety of holiday homes among cypress trees. A total of sixty freestanding units, duplexes, and row houses were all planned following the same design principles. Consequently, they are unified in materiality, color, and form. The composition of the floor plans is based on a square grid, but each unit is attuned to the specific topography, views of the landscape, entrance situation, and adjacencies. For that reason, the modular ordering system is barely perceptible. The colony has no fences. Narrow paths and steep stairs lead to the houses and continue past them over the hill. The concrete walls with inlaid quarry stone are one of Mangiarotti's trademarks. They turn up in all of the houses and border the swimming pool at the foot of the hill.

CINQUANT'ANNI
DI PITTURA VERONESE
1580-1630

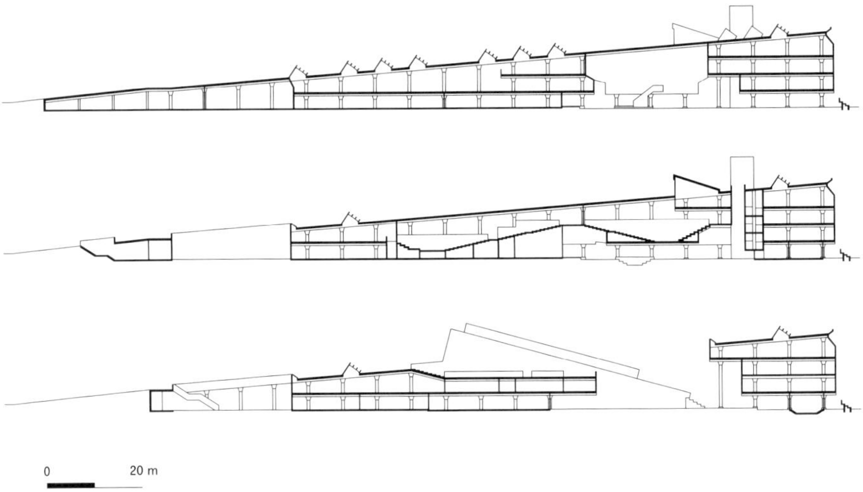

1971–76

LUIGI PELLEGRIN

ISTITUTO PER GEOMETRI E LICEO SCIENTIFICO
PISA, VIA ENRICO BETTI

This gigantic wedge contains a school: on one end it intersects with the ground, and on the other it is four stories high. In several different locations, cutouts interrupt the wedge's contours. The school's defining element is its roof. Pellegrin's attempts to have it integrated in Pisa's network of streets were futile, and at present only a small part of it is accessible. The sloped surface is supported by a field of regularly spaced columns, and from certain vantage points the load-bearing structure resembles a bridge. The open spaces under the school are remarkable, but have become an unused, pigeon-filled no-man's-land.

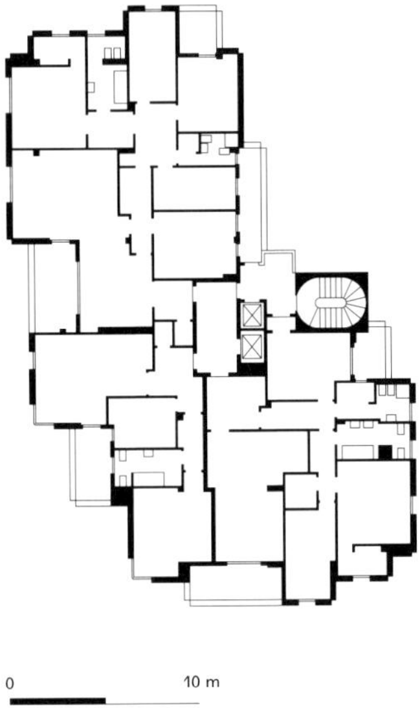

1972

ANGELO MANGIAROTTI

APARTMENT BUILDING
MONZA, VIA DEGLI ARTIGIANELLI

Mangiarotti employs the same basic principles as he did in his design of the apartment building on Via Quadronno [→**154**]: a reinforced concrete frame clad in a modular curtain-wall facade with a free arrangement of opaque and transparent elements. In this case, however, the components used in the curtain-wall facade are not of wood, but of prefabricated concrete panels. They give the impression that the exterior walls bear loads, but a closer look reveals that the walls stop short of the ground. The staggered loggias also make it clear that the elements are not part of the structural concept. Unlike at the apartment building on Via Quadronno, where the arrangement of the facades was determined in consultation with the occupants, here Mangiarotti only took aesthetic considerations into account.

danza

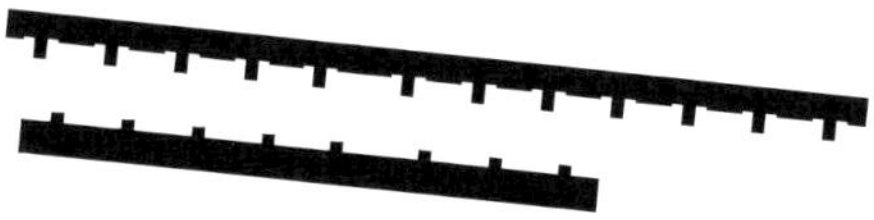

M 1:5000

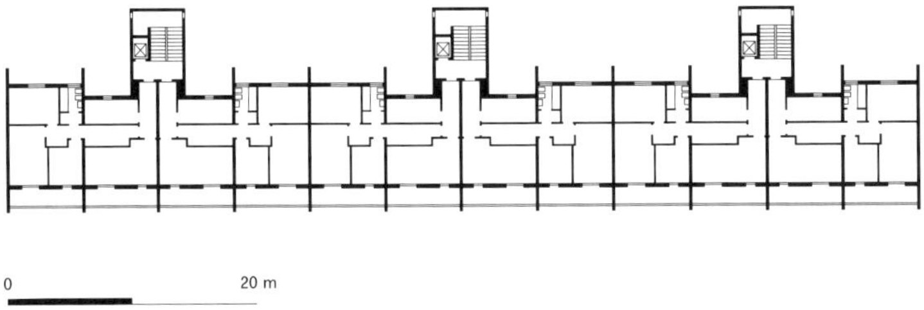

GABRIELLA PADOVANO, CESARE BLASI, UGO LA PIETRA, ALBERTO SEASSARO

HOUSING COMPLEX
VIMODRONE, VIA FIUME

1973–78

The design of this subsidized housing complex on the edge of Milan carries serial architecture to an extreme. The rigorous concept for the two apartment blocks—the first measures three hundred meters, the second, two hundred—stipulated a long succession of a single element. Immediately following completion of the project, the journal *L'architettura* praised its "unified skyline." The orientation of the longer of the two structures is puzzling: the terraces of this six-story block face north. In photos taken when the buildings were under construction, exposed concrete surfaces are dominant, but the louvered enclosures added since then have altered the appearance. The red garage doors accentuate the repetition and draw attention to the vanishing point. Can the building really be as long as it seems?

15

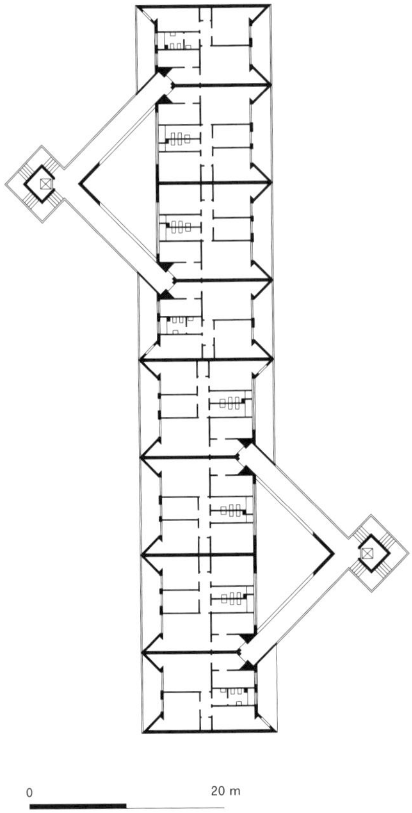

1974–83

GUIDO CANELLA

HOUSING COMPLEX
BOLLATE, VIA VINCENZO ATTIMO

Like the housing complex in Vimodrone [→**310**], the one in Bollate consists of a long, multi-story block and a smaller neighbor. Aspects of brutalism are discernible in both projects, but their formal vocabularies and overall structure are fundamentally different. In this design, Canella experiments with shifts in scale, as well as with monumentality and symbolism. Open stair towers modeled in high relief are spaced evenly on alternate sides of the 300-meter-long block. Huge gables between the stair towers make reference to local agrarian structures. Concrete gables were also added at the ends of the building, but they do not contain inhabitable spaces: they are merely roof-shaped caps.

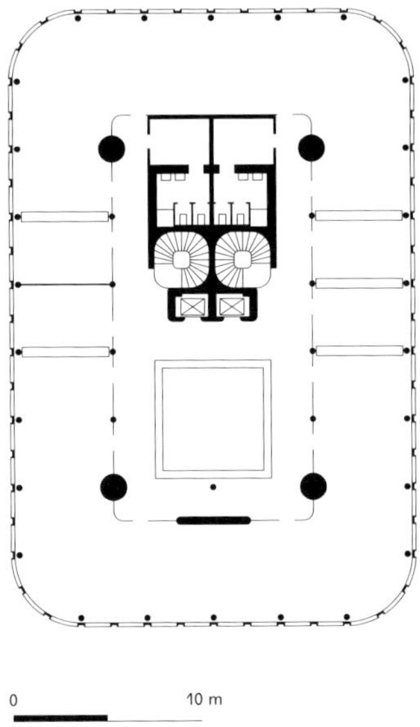

1976–78

ANGELO MANGIAROTTI

SNAIDERO FURNITURE FACTORY
MAJANO, VIALE RINO SNAIDERO 15

In 1976, an earthquake destroyed parts of this factory, and Mangiarotti was asked to design a new exhibition hall, a cafeteria, and the idiosyncratic office building depicted here. Perched above a stone plinth, it brings to mind the nineteen-sixties vision of the future developed by Japanese *metabolists*. But from the abstract concept to the detailing, it is without a doubt an authentic Mangiarotti building. The load-bearing structure consists of four hefty columns topped off by a reinforced concrete grille from which the office levels are suspended. The panels sheathing the exterior walls are made of two layers of fiberglass-reinforced plastic. All four sides of the curtain-wall facade are punctuated by oval windows reminiscent of portholes. The top floor only receives daylight through skylights.

DE GIROLAMI
Snaidero ti da
10 anni
di garanzia
snaidero
CUCINE PER LA VITA
248
snaidero
CUCINE PER LA VITA

snaidero

M 1:5000

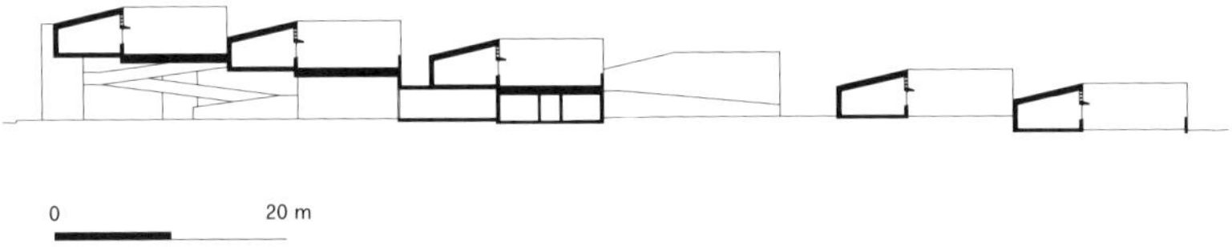

0 20 m

1976–79

GIUSEPPE GAMBIRASIO, GIORGIO ZENONI

RESIDENTIAL DISTRICT

BERGAMO, VIA CARDUCCI, VIA GOETHE, VIA ZENONI

At first glance this project appears to be a classical courtyard-house development. Aspects of the design bring to mind Jørn Utzon's houses in Fredensborg, Denmark. Gambirasio and Zenoni's residential district in Bergamo occupies a flat site. The single-story atrium houses are positioned atop a sloped platform—an artificial hillside, so to speak. This platform is supported by a raw concrete structure, which also accommodates the garage and storage. Yet there are also vast unprogrammed areas, or, in other words, residual spaces. In several locations scattered throughout the development, ramps and stairs lead down to the substructure. In the valley—on the southern edge—the dense network of paths intersects with the public realm.

DAL 380
AL 406

CAFFE'
LAVIN
KEBAB
PIZZA
PANINOTECA
BIRRERIA

436

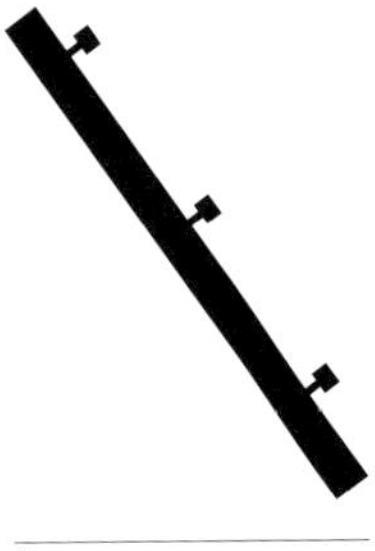

M 1:5000

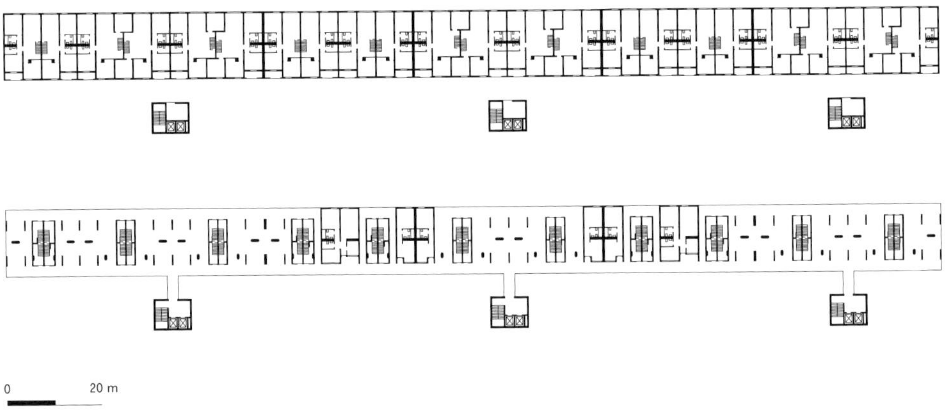

0 20 m

1976–79

GINO VALLE

APARTMENT BLOCK
UDINE, VIA RICCARDO DI GIUSTO

In his design of this subsidized apartment block employing a prefabricated construction system and containing one hundred units, Valle slits open the building massing to create sheltered outdoor spaces that run the entire length of the building. On the east side he set three stair towers in front of the long, rectangular building. These towers lead to the open levels, and, from there, to the entrances to the apartments. The open levels were envisioned as collective spaces: the horizontal and vertical circulation spaces have orange surfaces, while the publicly accessible spaces are coated in red. The exterior walls of the apartments, in contrast, are green. These photos were taken in May of 2000. Shortly thereafter the arresting color scheme succumbed to a new one. Now the building is cloaked in cool shades of blue and gray.

ALBINI & HELG

FRANCO ALBINI
∗1905 in Robbiate, †1977 in Milan. Studied architecture at the Politecnico in Milan; graduated in 1929. In the nineteen-thirties, he designed numerous exhibitions and items of furniture and built several rationalist housing complexes. After the war he moved away from strict geometry and spareness in favor of a moderate rationalism. His youth hostel in Cervinia—a log cabin on stone pillars—could even be considered a paradigm of neorealism. Albini taught at the IUAV in Venice, at the Politecnico in Turin and from 1963 to 1977 at the Politecnico in Milan.

FRANCA HELG
∗1920 in Milan, †1989 in Milan. Studied architecture at the Politecnico in Milan; graduated in 1945. Worked for BBPR; beginning in 1952, she formed a partnership with Franco Albini. In addition to her work as architect, Helg also achieved success as a furniture and lamp designer. Like Albini, she first taught in Venice, and beginning in 1963, at the Politecnico in Milan.

- AMENDOLA SUBWAY STATION, MILAN, 1962–65 →**202**

SELECTED BIBLIOGRAPHY

Domus № 438, May 1966
Architectural Forum January – February 1968
New Directions in Italian Architecture. Vittorio Gregotti. George Braziller, New York 1968
L'architettura, cronache e storia № 288, October 1979
Franco Albini. Centro Di, Florence 1979
Domus № 729, Itinerario 70: "Albini e Milano," July – August 1991
The Places of Franco Albini. Electa, Milan 2006

SELECTED WORK

Rifugio Pirovano, Cervinia, Strada Funivie, 1948–52 [→italomodern 2, **16**]
Palazzo Bianco Museum, Genoa, Via Garibaldi 11, 1949–51
Residential district (with BBPR, Ignazio Gardella et al.), Cesate, Villaggio I.N.A., 1950–54
Civic administration building, Genoa, Via Garibaldi 9, above Palazzo Tursi, 1950–63
Museum of the Treasury of San Lorenzo, Genoa, Piazza San Lorenzo, 1952–56
Department store, Rome, Piazza Fiume, 1957–61

ASNAGO & VENDER

MARIO ASNAGO
∗1896 in Barlassina, †1981 in Monza.

CLAUDIO VENDER
∗1904 in Milan, †1986 in Saronno.

Both architects studied at the Accademia di Brera and at the Politecnico in Milan; they ran a firm together from 1925 to 1971. Asnago & Vender's extensive oeuvre in Milan alone comprises more than fifty buildings, mostly office and apartment buildings in the heart of the city. From 1947 to 1956, they realized several projects right next to Torre Velasca. The apartment building on Piazza Sant'Ambrogio (1948) also has a prominent neighbor: it adjoins Caccia Dominioni's own house and studio (1947–51). Asnago & Vender paid special attention to their facades—in many of their projects they used stone cladding or combinations of stone and exposed brick-masonry; by employing slight shifts and a variety of window formats they created subtle building envelopes.

- MIXED-USE BUILDING, MILAN, 1961–64 →**184**

SELECTED BIBLIOGRAPHY

Domus № 688, Itinerario 29: "Asnago/Vender e Milano," November 1987
Asnago e Vender. Architetture e progetti 1925–1970. Skira, Milan 1999

SELECTED WORK

Mixed-use buildings in close proximity to Torre Velasca, Milan, Via Velasca 4, 1947–52; Via Paolo da Cannobbio 33, 1949; Via Albricci 10, 1953–56
Apartment building, Milan, Piazza Sant'Ambrogio 14, 1948
Mixed-use building, Milan, Via Lanzone 4, 1950–53
Addition to Casa Conti, Barlassina, Viale Trieste 29, 1958
Mixed-use building, Milan, Corso Sempione 75, 1961
Mixed-use building, Milan, Via della Signora 2A, 1966–70 [→italomodern 2, **378**]
Sant'Angelo, Rozzano, Viale Liguria 47, 1967–72 [→italomodern 2, **406**]

CARLO AYMONINO

∗1926 in Rome, †2010 in Rome. Studied architecture at La Sapienza in Rome; graduated in 1950. That same year he joined a group of architects including Ludovico Quaroni and Mario Ridolfi to take part in the design of the Tiburtino district—the built manifesto of neorealism. In the nineteen-sixties, he increasingly turned his attention to simple geometry—for example, sharp-edged building massing from which round staircases were cut, or circular recesses such as at the mixed-use building in Savona (1963–66). At the school campus in Pesaro (1970–84), primary geometric shapes—circles, squares and triangles—play an especially important role. Aymonino taught in Rome, Palermo, and Venice. From 1959 to 1964, he was on the editorial board of *Casabella*.

- GALLARATESE HOUSING COMPLEX (WITH ALDO ROSSI), 1967–74 →**250**

SELECTED BIBLIOGRAPHY

Lotus international № 7, 1970
GA 45. Housing Complex at the Gallaratese Quarter. Tokyo 1977
GA Document. Special Issue 1970–80, Tokyo 1980
Milano. Maurizio Grandi, Attilio Pracchi. Zanichelli, Bologna 1980
Modern Architecture. Manfredo Tafuri, Francesco Dal Co. Rizzoli, New York 1986
Italian Architecture: 1945–1985. Francesco Dal Co, Sergio Polano. a+u Extra Edition, Tokyo 1988
Carlo Aymonino. Giancarlo Priori. Zanichelli, Bologna 1990
Guida all'architettura italiana del Novecento. Sergio Polano. Electa, Milan 1991
Milano. Architectural Guide. Allemandi, Turin 1999
Milano. Giuliana Gramigna, Sergio Mazza. Ulrico Hoepli, Milan 2001

SELECTED WORK

Quartiere Tiburtino, Rome, Via Tiburtina, Via Diego Angeli, 1950–52
Chamber of Commerce, Carrara, Piazza 2 Giugno 16, 1956–60
Apartment building, Rome, Via Arbia 21, 1960–61
Mixed-use building, Savona, Piazza Armando Diaz, 1963–66
Campus Scolastico, Pesaro, Via Nanterre 1, 1970–84 [→italomodern 2, **478**]

MARIO BACCIOCCHI

∗1902 in Fiorenzuola d'Arda, †1974 in Milan. Studied architecture at the Politecnico in Milan; graduated in 1925. Bacciocchi created the standardized Agip gas stations with emblematic sweeping cantilevers that were erected throughout Italy during the fifties. In 1952, for the oil company Eni—which owns Agip—he developed a master plan for a company town whose name is derived from the word "methane": Metanopoli. He designed a motel, a laboratory building, the sports center, several apartment buildings, and the Chiesa di Santa Barbara for this newly established locality on the southeast edge of Milan. The "gas-station architect" built four other churches, including Sant'Angela Merici in Milan (1957–59).

- AGIP GAS STATION, MILAN, 1954–60 →**62**

SELECTED BIBLIOGRAPHY

Domus № 811, Itinerario 152: "Stazioni di Servizio," January 1999

SELECTED WORK

Torre Locatelli, Milan, Piazza della Repubblica, Via Vittor Pisani, 1936–39
Standardized gas stations for Agip, 1953–60
Laboratory building, Metanopoli, Viale De Gasperi, Via Fabiani, 1953–54
Motel, Metanopoli, Piazzale Supercortemaggiore, 1954
Chiesa di Santa Barbara, Metanopoli, Piazza Santa Barbara, 1955
Chiesa di Sant'Angela Merici, Milan, Via Cardinale Cagliero 26, 1957–59

BBPR

GIAN LUIGI BANFI
∗1910 in Milan, †1945 in Mauthausen.

LODOVICO BARBIANO DI BELGIOJOSO
∗1909 in Milan, †2004 in Milan.

ENRICO PERESSUTTI
∗1908 in Pinzano di Tagliamento, †1976 in Milan.

ERNESTO NATHAN ROGERS
∗1909 in Trieste, †1969 in Gardone.

All four studied architecture at the Politecnico in Milan; in 1932, they established BBPR. With their designs of the nineteen-thirties—such as the ten-story Feltrinelli Building (a mixed-use structure) in Milan and the sanatorium in Legnano—they became important representatives of rationalism. After the war (following the death of Gian Luigi Banfi, the three remaining principals continued to call themselves BBPR) they practiced a moderate rationalism and attempted to forge a link to regional building traditions and incorporate context in their architectural vocabulary. Torre Velasca, in Milan's central business district, was BBPR's key work. The project elicited hostile reactions far beyond Italy's borders, especially from advocates of dogmatic modernism at the CIAM Congress in Otterlo (1959), where Ernesto Nathan Rogers presented it. In addition to his work as an architect, Rogers played another major role in the field: he emerged as an influential theoretician and, from 1953 to 1964, headed the magazine *Casabella*. Beginning in 1962, he taught at the Politecnico in Milan.

• TORRE VELASCA, MILAN, 1950–58 →**42**

SELECTED BIBLIOGRAPHY

L'architettura, cronache e storia № 40, February 1959
Casabella № 232, October 1959
CIAM '59 in Otterlo. Documents of Modern Architecture. Karl Krämer, Stuttgart 1961
The New Architecture of Europe. G. E. Kidder Smith. World Publishing, Cleveland 1961
New Italian Architecture. Alberto Galardi. Praeger, New York 1967
New Directions in Italian Architecture. Vittorio Gregotti. George Braziller, New York 1968
Twentieth Century Architecture. Dennis Sharp. Heinemann/Secker & Warburg, London 1972
28/78 Architettura. Domus, Milan 1979
Das Ende der Zuversicht. Wolfgang Pehnt. Siedler, Berlin 1983
BBPR. Architecture 1932–1987. Italian Cultural Institute, New York 1988
Italian Architecture: 1945–1985. Francesco Dal Co, Sergio Polano. a+u Extra Edition, Tokyo 1988
Guida all'architettura italiana del Novecento. Sergio Polano. Electa, Milan 1991
L'architettura del Novecento. Cesare de'Seta. Garzanti, Milan 1992
BBPR. Serena Maffioletti. Zanichelli, Bologna 1994
Domus № 797, Itinerario 138: "BBPR e Milano," October 1997
The Sense of History. Ernesto Nathan Rogers. Unicopli, Milan 1999
Milano. Architectural Guide. Allemandi, Turin 1999
BBPR. La Torre Velasca. Federico Brunetti. Alinea, Florence 1999
2G № 15, "Postwar Italian Architecture 1944–1960." Gustavo Gili, Barcelona 2000
Milano. Giuliana Gramigna, Sergio Mazza. Ulrico Hoepli, Milan 2001

SELECTED WORK

Mixed-use building, Milan, Piazza della Repubblica, Via Manin, 1934–35
Canadian Pavilion, Venice, Giardini della Biennale, 1956–57
Mixed-use building, Turin, Corso Francia, Piazza Statuto, 1957–59 [→italomodern 2, **184**]
Apartment buildings, Milan, Via dei Chiostri 1, Via Cavalieri del Santo Sepolcro 10–12, Via Pontaccio 8–10, 1961–70 [→italomodern 2, **260**, **262**]
Olivetti office building, Barcelona, Ronda de la Universitat, 1964–65
Condominio, Madonna di Campiglio, Pian dei Frari, 1965–67 [→italomodern 2, **354**]

PIERO BOTTONI

*1903 in Milan, †1973 in Milan. Studied architecture at the Politecnico in Milan; graduated in 1926. Bottoni co-founded *MIAR*, *Movimento Italiano per l'Architettura Razionale*, in 1930; that same year he took part in the CIAM Congress in Brussels. In 1933, he co-authored the Charter of Athens (CIAM 4). With the design of Villa Dello Strongolo in Livorno (1934–35) he made his mark early: the building became a paradigm of *Razionalismo*. In addition to designs for furniture, Bottoni also worked on projects at the urban scale, including a land-use plan for Aosta Valley (1936–37) and the conception of satellite cities in Milan's hinterland. Beginning in 1945, he headed the planning of the new Milanese district QT8—an experimental residential district laid out in conjunction with the city's 8th Triennale. His work on Monte Stella, an artificial hill made of war debris, on the expansive QT8 grounds began in 1953. He renovated and converted the Palazzo di Renata di Francia to the new seat of the university in Ferrara with great sensitivity. Bottoni taught at the engineering faculty in Trieste from 1954 to 1965 and at the Politecnico in Milan from 1964 to 1971.

- CITY HALL, SESTO SAN GIOVANNI, 1961–71 →**198**

SELECTED BIBLIOGRAPHY

L'architettura, cronache e storia № 146, December 1967
Piero Bottoni. Opera completa. Fabbri, Milan 1990
Domus № 721, Itinerario 62: "Bottoni e Milano," November 1990
Piero Bottoni. The School of Milan. Electa, Milan 2010

SELECTED WORK

Villa Dello Strongolo, Livorno, Via Diomede Buonamici 15, 1934–35
Residential district, Milan, QT8, 1945–57
Exhibition pavilion, Milan, QT8, Via Giuseppe Pogatschnig 34, 1951
Apartment block, Milan, Corso Sempione 33, 1953–56
Monte Stella, Milan, QT8, 1953–70
Conversion and renovation of Palazzo di Renata di Francia, Ferrara, Via Savonarola 9, 1960–64

LUIGI CACCIA DOMINIONI

*1913 in Milan. Studied architecture at the Politecnico in Milan; graduated in 1936. Dominioni teamed up with Livio and Pier Giacomo Castiglioni for the design of several competition projects, interiors, flatware services, and even radios before setting up his own office in 1945. During a period lasting some sixty years and marked by all-consuming dedication to his work, Caccia Dominioni devised, in his own words, "hundreds of projects." Presence on the building site and the painstaking implementation of his designs were more important to him than taking part in the contemporary discourse. With his designs of elegant ceramic facades he established a school of his own: the office building on Via Savona and the orphanage on Via Calatafimi mark the beginning of his use of the material. He also designed furniture, lamps, and other accessories—for example, door handles—for use in his residential work. In 1947, in order to serially produce their own designs, Caccia Dominioni, Ignazio Gardella, and Corrado Corradi Dell'Acqua established the firm *Azucena*.

- CONVENTO E ISTITUTO DELLA BEATA VERGINE ADDOLORATA, MILAN, 1948–54 →**18**
- SCHOOL (WITH LIVIO CASTIGLIONI, PIER GIACOMO CASTIGLIONI), VIMERCATE, 1948–60 →**22**
- LORO & PARISINI OFFICE BUILDING, MILAN, 1951–57 →**46**
- MIXED-USE BUILDINGS, MILAN, 1953–59 →**54**
- APARTMENT BUILDING, MILAN, 1955–57 →**68**
- APARTMENT BUILDING, MILAN, 1956–59 →**76**
- MIXED-USE BUILDING, MILAN, 1957–64 →**118**
- RESIDENCE, MILAN, 1958–64 →**122**
- APARTMENT BUILDING, MILAN, 1959–63 →**122**
- APARTMENT BUILDING, MILAN, 1960–61 →**150**
- CONVENTO DI SAN ANTONIO FRATI MINORI, MILAN, 1960–63 →**158**
- HOLIDAY HOMES, PINETA DI ARENZANO, 1961–63 →**180**
- OFFICE BUILDINGS, MILAN, 1963–66 →**208**

SELECTED BIBLIOGRAPHY

Casabella № 207, September – October 1955
Casabella № 230, August 1959
Domus № 403, June 1963
The New Architecture of Europe. G. E. Kidder Smith. Piper, Munich 1964
Milano. Maurizio Grandi, Attilio Pracchi. Zanichelli, Bologna 1980

Casabella № 508, December 1984
Il Condominio a Milano. Di Baio Editore, Milan 1987
Guida all'architettura italiana del Novecento. Sergio Polano. Electa, Milan 1991
Milano Moderna. Fulvio Irace. Federico Motta Editore, Milan 1996
Luigi Caccia Dominioni. Maria Antonietta Crippa. Testo & Immagine, Turin 1996
Domus № 790, Itinerario 131: "Caccia Dominioni e Milano," February 1997
Milano. Giuliana Gramigna, Sergio Mazza. Ulrico Hoepli, Milan 2001
d'Architettura № 19, November 2002
Luigi Caccia Dominioni. Stile di Caccia. Marsilio, Venice 2003
La Pineta di Arenzano. Marco Franzone, Gerolamo Patrone. Skira, Milan 2010

SELECTED WORK

Casa Caccia Dominioni, Milan, Piazza Sant'Ambrogio 16, 1947–51
Office building, Milan, Piazza Velasca 7–9, 1963–70
Library, Morbegno, Piazza Aldo Moro, 1965–66 [→italomodern 2, **350**]
San Biagio, Monza, Via Carlo Prina 19, 1965–69 [→italomodern 2, **360**]
San Felice residential district (with Vico Magistretti), Segrate, Via San Bovio, Strada Anulare, 1967–75 [→italomodern 2, **422**]
Apartment building, Genoa, Corso Aurelio Saffi 36, Salita dei Sassi, 1977
Faculty building, Milan, Via Bernardo Ugo Secondo, Via Celeste Clericetti, 1996–97

GUIDO CANELLA

∗1931 in Bucharest, †2009 in Milan. Studied architecture at the Politecnico in Milan; graduated in 1959. He was assistant professor under Giuseppe Samonà in Venice and later under Ernesto N. Rogers in Milan. In 1970, he was appointed full professor in Milan. Beginning in 1957, Canella wrote numerous articles for the magazine *Casabella*. He was publisher of the magazines *Hinterland* (1978–85) and *Zodiac* (1989–99). A significant number of Canella's buildings are located just outside of Milan. He was, for example, responsible for the design of most of the public buildings of the satellite city Pieve Emanuele: city hall, two schools, preschool, social center, piazza, church, and market (1968–83). These projects allowed him to experiment, and he worked with bold massing and emblematic objects.

- HOUSING COMPLEX, BOLLATE, 1974–83 →**312**

SELECTED BIBLIOGRAPHY

Casabella № 437, June 1978
Milano. Maurizio Grandi, Attilio Pracchi. Zanichelli, Bologna 1980
Domus № 635, January 1983
Guido Canella. Katuyouki Suzuky. Zanichelli, Bologna 1983
Guido Canella. Architetture 1957–1987. Enrico Bordogna. Electa, Milan 1987
Italian Architecture: 1945–1985. Francesco Dal Co, Sergio Polano. a+u Extra Edition, Tokyo 1988
Guida all'architettura italiana del Novecento. Sergio Polano. Electa, Milan 1991

SELECTED WORK

City hall, Segrate, Via 25 Aprile, 1963–67
Municipal facilities, Pieve Emanuele, Via Johann Strauss, Via Riccardo Zandonai, 1968–81
Civic center, Pieve Emanuele, Via Viquarterio, 1971–83
Preschool, Opera, Via San Bernardo, 1972–76
City hall, Pioltello, Via Carlo Cattaneo 1, 1976–80 [→italomodern 2, **536**]

CAPPAI & MAINARDIS

IGINIO CAPPAI
∗1932 in Venice, † 1999. Studied architecture in Venice; graduated in 1962. Assistant professor under Franco Albini and later under Ignazio Gardella at the IUAV in Venice.

PIETRO MAINARDIS
∗1935 in Venice, † 2007. Studied architecture in Venice; graduated in 1960. Assistant professor under Ignazio Gardella.

Cappai & Mainardis set up an office together in 1962. They prepared designs for numerous competitions, for example, for the new city hall in Amsterdam (1963); for the restructuring of Varna, Bulgaria (1966); and for the new House of Representatives in Rome (1967). In 1967, they began to design both the Casa Gialla in Mira and the Olivetti Hotel in Ivrea. Most of their other buildings were erected in and around Venice.

- CASA GIALLA, MIRA, 1967–69 →**240**
- OLIVETTI HOTEL, IVREA, 1967–75 →**262**
- SCHOOL, MIRA, ORIAGO, 1968–70 →**268**

SELECTED BIBLIOGRAPHY
Casabella № 350/351, July – August 1970
Casabella № 377, May 1973
L'architettura, cronache e storia № 249, July 1976
Casabella № 422, February 1977
Bauen + Wohnen № 2/3, February – March 1977
GA Document, Special Issue 1970–1980, Tokyo 1980
Guida all'architettura italiana del Novecento. Sergio Polano. Electa, Milan 1991
Olivetti Builds. Modern Architecture in Ivrea. Patrizia Bonifazio, Paolo Scrivano. Skira, Milan 2001
Cappai e Mainardis. Laboratorio veneziano. Luigi Pavan. Testo & Immagine, Turin 2004

SELECTED WORK
Yacht club, Venice Lido, Lungomare Guglielmo Marconi 52, 1979–81
Post office, Mira, Via Enrico Toti, 1983–85
Housing complex, Venice, Sacca Fisola, Calle Larga Mario Brunetti, 1985–99

ENRICO CASTIGLIONI

∗1914 in Busto Arsizio, † 2000 in Busto Arsizio. Studied civil engineering at the Politecnico in Milan; graduated in 1937. A proponent of "dynamic architecture," he made his mark with bold constructions and elaborate shell structures. His competition project for the new central station in Naples (1954) was widely acclaimed and was on the cover of the first issue of Bruno Zevi's magazine *L'architettura* (May–June 1955). Though most of them remained on paper, his designs of churches provided an important field of experimentation with respect to complex geometries and the gentle orchestration of light. Of particular note is his project for the Syracuse cathedral (1957). His built work is located in or near Busto Arsizio.

- SCHOOL, BUSTO ARSIZIO, 1957–58 →**102**
- ISTITUTO TECNICO INDUSTRIALE E ISTITUTO PROFESSIONALE DI STATO, BUSTO ARSIZIO, CASTELLANZA, 1960–64 →**164**

SELECTED BIBLIOGRAPHY
L'architettura, cronache e storia № 60, October 1960
Baukunst und Werkform № 1, January 1961
New Architecture in the World. Udo Kultermann. Thames & Hudson, London 1966
New Italian Architecture. Alberto Galardi. Praeger, New York 1967
Architektur der Gegenwart. Udo Kultermann. Holle, Baden-Baden 1967
Twentieth Century Architecture. Dennis Sharp. Heinemann/Secker & Warburg, London 1972
28/78 Architettura. Domus, Milan 1979

SELECTED WORK
Residential district (with Franco Albini, BBPR, Ignazio Gardella, et al.), Cesate, Villaggio I.N.A., 1950–54
Catholic community center, Busto Arsizio, Via Antoni Pozzi 7, 1954–55
Restaurant on Lago Maggiore, Lisanza, Via Lario, 1958–62
Residential district, Busto Arsizio, Via Giotto, Piazzale Gabriele D'Annunzio, 1959
School, Gorla Minore, Parco Durini, 1959–63
Church, Gorla Minore, Piazza Giovanni XXIII, 1962–66

LIVIO, PIER GIACOMO AND ACHILLE CASTIGLIONI

LIVIO CASTIGLIONI
∗1911 in Milan, †1979 in Milan.

PIER GIACOMO CASTIGLIONI
∗1913 in Milan, † in Milan.

ACHILLE CASTIGLIONI
∗1918 in Milan, †2002 in Milan.

All three brothers studied architecture at the Politecnico in Milan. In 1938, Livio and Pier Giacomo set up their practice in Milan. Following his graduation in 1944, Achille Castiglioni joined his brothers' office. From the start, in addition to architecture and urban planning projects, the office focused on industrial design. The brothers designed furniture and items of daily use, including a radio with Bakelite housing. In 1956, all three were involved in the establishment of the *Associazione per il Disegno Industriale*. But four years prior to that, Livio Castiglioni had left the office to concentrate on industrial design. In addition to their design objects, Pier Giacomo and Achille also produced numerous interiors, exhibitions, showrooms and trade-fair pavilions.

- SCHOOL (WITH LUIGI CACCIA DOMINIONI), VIMERCATE, 1948–60 →**22**
- CHIESA SAN GABRIELE ARCANGELO IN MATER DEI, MILAN, 1956–60 →**78**

SELECTED BIBLIOGRAPHY
Casabella № 224, February 1959
Achille Castiglioni. Paolo Ferrari. Electa, Milan 1984
Italian Architecture: 1945–1985. Francesco Dal Co, Sergio Polano. a+u Extra Edition, Tokyo 1988
Guida all'architettura italiana del Novecento. Sergio Polano. Electa, Milan 1991
Milano. Giuliana Gramigna, Sergio Mazza. Ulrico Hoepli, Milan 2001
Achille Castiglioni 1918–2002. Sergio Polano. Electa, Milan 2007

SELECTED WORK
Torre della Permanente, Milan, Via Turati 34, 1949–53

CELLI & TOGNON

CARLO CELLI
∗1936 in Trieste.

LUCIANO CELLI
∗1940 in Trieste.

DARIO TOGNON
∗1936 in Pula, †2008 in Trieste.

All three studied architecture in Venice; they set up their office together in 1964. The following year they were commissioned to design their first major building: Trieste's new hospital. The office implemented it in cooperation with Luciano Semerani and Gigetta Tamaro. Shortly thereafter they realized two very different churches, one in Trieste's dense urban fabric (Santa Teresa, 1968–72) and the other on a hillside in Zindis (1969–73), a fishing village. In 1970, they began work on their most important building: the Rozzol Melara housing complex.

- ROZZOL MELARA HOUSING COMPLEX, TRIESTE, 1970–83 →**288**

SELECTED BIBLIOGRAPHY
Casabella № 419, November 1976
Casabella № 437, June 1978
Edilizia popolare a Trieste. Flavia Castro. Lint, Trieste 1984
Italian Architecture: 1945–1985. Francesco Dal Co, Sergio Polano. a+u Extra Edition, Tokyo 1988
Guida all'architettura italiana del Novecento. Sergio Polano. Electa, Milan 1991

SELECTED WORK
Cattinara Hospital (with Semerani & Tamaro), Trieste, Strada di Fiume, 1965–83
Church Santa Teresa, Trieste, Via Matteotti, Via Manzoni, 1968–72
Church San Matteo, Zindis, Strada per Lazzaretto, 1969–73
Supermarket, Trieste, Via San Marco, Viale dei Campi Elisi, 1972–74
Orphanage, Gradisca d'Isonzo, Via Eulambio, 1976–80

LUIGI CARLO DANERI

*1900 in Borgo Fornari, †1972 in Trieste. Studied in Genoa and Rome; graduated in 1923. Daneri opened his office in Genoa in 1929 and was one of the key figures of the city's modern movement. The influence of Le Corbusier is discernible in several of his projects: his design of a building for the fascist party—Casa Littoria Rionale (1936–38)—is reminiscent of Villa Savoye, and the apartment block on Via Buonvicini (1954–56) brings to mind the Unité projects. As early as 1934, Daneri began to implement his designs of large housing complexes, and after the war he built numerous projects for the *INA-Casa* social housing program in Genoa.

- BOATYARD (WITH PIER LUIGI NERVI), SAN MICHELE DI PAGANA, 1948–50 →**14**
- FORTE QUEZZI HOUSING COMPLEX, GENOA, 1956–68 →**86**

SELECTED BIBLIOGRAPHY

Italy Builds. G. E. Kidder Smith. The Architectural Press, London 1955

L'architettura, cronache e storia № 56, June 1960

Casabella № 325, April – June 1968

Art & Landscape of Italy. Centro Di, Florence 1972

Modern Architecture. Manfredo Tafuri, Francesco Dal Co. Rizzoli, New York 1986

Domus № 718, Itinerario 59: "Daneri e Genova," July – August 1990

Guida all'architettura italiana del Novecento. Sergio Polano. Electa, Milan 1991

Luigi Carlo Daneri. Razionalista a Genova. Testo & Immagine, Turin 2003

Genova 900. L'architettura del Movimento Moderno. Testo & Immagine, Turin 2004

Genova. Guide to modern architecture. Alinea Editrice, Florence 2004

Genoa. 100 Years of Architecture. De Ferrari, Genoa 2004

SELECTED WORK

Casa Littoria Rionale, Genoa, Piazza Sturla 3, 1936–38

Office building, Genoa, Via Varese 2, 1949–58

Residential district, Genoa, Viale Bernabò Brea, 1950–54

Apartment block, Genoa, Via Buonvicini 21–39, 1954–56

Holiday flats, San Remo, Ospedaletti, Via Aurelia Levante, 1961–72 [→italomodern 2, **264**]

MARCELLO D'OLIVO

*1921 in Udine, †1991 in Udine. Studied architecture in Venice; graduated in 1947. D'Olivo is considered one of the main proponents of postwar Italy's *Tendenza organica*; the critic Bruno Zevi called him the "Italian Wright." As city planner he designed the resort town Lignano Pineta (1952–63) with a spiral-shaped street layout. He participated in numerous international competitions and built a hospital in Amman, Jordan (1958–60). Beginning in the nineteen-sixties, he worked on several projects in Africa, including a stadium in Libreville, Gabon (1970–74). In the nineteen-eighties, D'Olivo increasingly turned his attention to urban fantasies and painting.

- VILLAGGIO DEL FANCIULLO, CAFETERIA, TRIESTE, OPICINA, 1950–57 →**38**
- HOLIDAY HOME, LIGNANO PINETA, 1954–55 →**58**

SELECTED BIBLIOGRAPHY

L'architettura, cronache e storia № 20, June 1957

The New Architecture of Europe. G. E. Kidder Smith. World Publishing, Cleveland 1961

New Architecture in the World. Udo Kultermann. Thames & Hudson, London 1966

New Italian Architecture. Alberto Galardi. Praeger, New York 1967

Architektur der Gegenwart. Udo Kultermann. Holle, Baden-Baden 1967

Italian Architecture: 1945–1985. Francesco Dal Co, Sergio Polano. a+u Extra Edition, Tokyo 1988

Guida all'architettura italiana del Novecento. Sergio Polano. Electa, Milan 1991

Marcello D'Olivo Architetto. Mazzotta, Milan 2002

Marcello D'Olivo. Il Villaggio del Fanciullo. Gaspari, Udine 2005

SELECTED WORK

Convent school, Trieste, Via Italo Svevo 34, 1949–52

Mixed-use building Il Treno, Lignano Pineta, Raggio dell'Ostro, 1952–60

Holidy home, Lignano Pineta, Arco del Maestrale, 1955–57

Cafeteria, Trieste, Via Carli 12, 1956–58

Apartment building, Grado, Largo San Grisogono 14, 1960–64

Unknown Soldier Monument, Baghdad, 1979–82

ANNIBALE FIOCCHI

*1915 in Milan, †2011 in Ivrea. Studied architecture at the Politecnico in Milan; graduated in 1939. From 1947 to 1954, Fiocchi headed Olivetti's planning department in Ivrea, and then established his own architecture practice in the same city. He maintained his close ties to Olivetti, both as consultant and as architect, for example, of the firm's new headquarters on Via Jervis, which he designed in cooperation with Gian Antonio Bernasconi and Marcello Nizzoli (1955–64). At the 9th Triennale of Milan (1951), Fiocchi received the Gold Medal for his design of Ivrea's Canton Vesco residential district (1949–54).

- OLIVETTI SUMMER CAMP, MARINA DI MASSA, 1950–56 →**34**

SELECTED BIBLIOGRAPHY

Bauen + Wohnen № 8, August 1956
L'architettura, cronache e storia № 54, April 1960
Itinerari Apuani di Architettura Moderna. Pietro Giorgieri. Alinea, Florence 1989
Olivetti Builds. Patrizia Bonifazio, Paolo Scrivano. Skira, Milan 2001

SELECTED WORK

Residential district (with Marcello Nizzoli), Ivrea, Via Gramsci, Via Galimberti, 1949–54
Olivetti office building (with Gian Antonio Bernasconi, Marcello Nizzoli), Milan, Via Clerici 4, 1950–54
Olivetti headquarters (with Gian Antonio Bernasconi, Marcello Nizzoli), Ivrea, Via Jervis 77, 1955–64
Residential district (with Marcello Nizzoli, Gian Mario Oliveri), Metanopoli, Via Caviaga, Via Fermi, 1956–57
Shoe factory, Varese, Viale Belforte 178, 1961–65

GABETTI & ISOLA

ROBERTO GABETTI
*1925 in Turin, †2000 in Turin. Studied architecture with Giovanni Muzio in Turin; graduated in 1949. Taught at the Politecnico in Turin for fifty years, initially as assistant professor, and, beginning in 1967, as full professor for architectural design.

AIMARO ISOLA
*1928 in Turin. Studied architecture with Carlo Mollino in Turin; graduated in 1952. Taught at the Politecnico in Turin beginning in 1953; he was named full professor for urban planning and architectural design in 1977.

In 1950, Gabetti & Isola set up an office together in Turin. After the publication of their Bottega d'Erasmo project—an apartment building with an antiquarian bookshop—in *Casabella* № 215 and Reyner Banham's response to the article (*The Architectural Review* № 47, 1958: "The Italian Retreat from Modern Architecture"), they were the talk of the town. Gabetti & Isola became proponents of *Neoliberty*, the short-lived movement of a young generation of architects who turned away from dogmatic modernism and sought a new understanding of tradition and history.

- RIDING HALL, TURIN, NICHELINO, 1959–60 →**128**
- CASA-ALBERGO ECA (WITH GIORGIO RAINERI), TURIN, 1964–68 →**214**
- OLIVETTI APARTMENT BUILDING, IVREA, 1968–74 →**272**

SELECTED BIBLIOGRAPHY

L'architettura, cronache e storia № 77, March 1962
New Italian Architecture. Alberto Galardi. Praeger, New York 1967
L'architettura, cronache e storia № 212/213, June – July 1973
Architetture olivettiane a Ivrea. Gangemi, Rome 1988
Gabetti e Isola. Paolo Zermani. Zanichelli, Bologna 1989

SELECTED WORK

Bottega d'Erasmo, Turin, Via Gaudenzio Ferrari 11, 1953–56
Centrale SIP, Mondovì, Via Giosuè Carducci, 1972–76 [→italomodern 2, **492**]
Apartment building, Sestrière, Via La Gleisa, 1976–78
Courthouse, Alba, Viale Torino, 1981–87

GIUSEPPE GAMBIRASIO

*1930 in Bergamo. Studied architecture in Milan and Venice; graduated in 1957. Assistant professor at departments headed by Albini, Samonà, Gardella, and Scarpa; beginning in 1981, full professor at the IUAV in Venice. From the very start, his projects demonstrated an adeptness at working in three dimensions and a penchant for experimentation, both in terms of conception and materiality: he created astonishing unprogrammed spaces such as the underworld at the residential districts in Bergamo (1976–79) and in Spotorno (1976–83) and experimented with translucent, fiber-reinforced plastic panels (La Felce mixed-use building, 1967) and with raw aluminum plate (apartment building in Calolziocorte, 1966) or with polyester-resin concrete coatings (preschool in Curno, 1969–72). Many of his buildings were developed in cooperation with Walter Barbero (*1941 in Rome, †2010 in Bergamo), Baran Ciagà (*1934 in Istanbul) and Giorgio Zenoni (*1935 in Genoa).

- APARTMENT BUILDING, CALOLZIOCORTE, 1966 →**226**
- MIXED-USE BUILDING (WITH WALTER BARBERO, GIORGIO ZENONI), BERGAMO, 1969–71 →**278**
- PRESCHOOL (WITH BARAN CIAGÀ), BERGAMO, CURNO, 1969–72 →**280**
- RESIDENTIAL DISTRICT (WITH GIORGIO ZENONI), BERGAMO, 1976–79 →**318**

SELECTED BIBLIOGRAPHY

L'architettura, cronache e storia № 184, February 1971
Casabella № 361, January 1972
Domus № 513, August 1972
werk № 10, October 1972
werk № 2, February 1973
L'architecture d'aujourd'hui № 166, March – April 1973
Casabella № 376, April 1973
Casabella № 386, February 1974
28/78 Architettura. Domus, Milan 1979
Domus № 615, March 1981
Gambirasio. Enrico Pinna. Sagep, Genoa 1987

SELECTED WORK

Mixed-use building (with Walter Barbero, Giorgio Zenoni), Bergamo, Via Borfuro, 1967

Residential complex (with Giorgio Zenoni), Spotorno, Via Giuseppe Verdi 11, 1976–83 [→Italomodern 2, **538**]

IGNAZIO GARDELLA

*1905 in Milan, †1999 in Oleggio. Studied engineering at the Politecnico in Milan; graduated in 1928. Studied architecture in Venice; graduated in 1949. His first realizations were carried out in cooperation with his father Arnaldo. He set up his own office in Milan in 1931. As an "undogmatic rationalist" he designed a tuberculosis clinic in Alessandria (1934–38) that was to become a paradigm of Italian rationalism. Yet the design contained a traditional element, a brick grille wall similar to those in the area's anonymous barns. His apartment buildings in Alessandria (1948–52) and in the Giardino d'Arcadia in Milan (1949–53) testify to a further step away from abstraction. In addition to his incredibly large architectural oeuvre, Gardella also engaged in the design of furniture. In 1947, Luigi Caccia Dominioni, Corrado Corradi Dell'Acqua, and Gardella established the firm *Azucena* to manufacture their own designs. As Italy's representatives, Gardella, Magistretti, De Carlo, and Rogers took part in the final CIAM Congress in Otterlo in 1959. Gardella taught at the IUAV in Venice from 1962 to 1975.

- APARTMENT BUILDING, ALESSANDRIA, 1948–52 →**16**
- HOLIDAY FLATS, PINETA DI ARENZANO, 1958–65 →**124**
- CHIESA SAN NICOLAO DELLA FLUE, MILAN, 1962–70 →**206**

SELECTED BIBLIOGRAPHY

Casabella № 199, December 1953 – January 1954
Casabella № 284, February 1964
Ignazio Gardella. Fabio Nonis, Sergio Boidi. Electa International, Milan 1986
Milano. Giuliana Gramigna, Sergio Mazza. Ulrico Hoepli, Milan 2001

SELECTED WORK

Outpatient Clinic, Alessandria, Via Gasparolo 2, 1934–38

Apartment building in the Giardino d'Arcadia, Milan, Via Paolo Marchiondi 7, 1949–53

Apartment building, Venice, Fondamenta Zattere allo Spirito Santo, 1953–58

City hall, Pordenone, Piazzetta Calderari, 1963–66 [→italomodern 2, **300**]

Faculty of Architecture, Genoa, Stradone di Sant'Agostino 37, 1975–89

VITTORIO GIORGINI

*1926 in Florence, †2010 in Florence. Giorgini studied architecture in Florence until 1957 and opened his office the following year. During this phase he was assistant professor under Leonardo Savioli. In 1969, he moved to New York and, beginning in 1971, taught at Pratt Institute. Five years later, Giorgini and a group of his students began work on the so-called Liberty Center in Upstate New York—a structure comparable to the holiday home in Baratti. But the funds did not suffice to complete the jellyfish-like figure; the imposing wire-mesh structure was later dismantled. In 1999, he returned to Florence. The FRAC Centre in Orléans, France, acquired a selection of Vittorio Giorgini's drawings and models for its collection.

- HEXAGON, BARATTI, 1957 →**96**
- HOLIDAY HOME, BARATTI, 1961–62 →**174**

SELECTED BIBLIOGRAPHY

Aujourd'hui № 53, May – June 1966
Topologia e Morfogenesi. Utopia e Crisi dell'Antinatura. Lara Vinca Masini. Edizioni La Biennale di Venezia, 1978
Spatiology. Vittorio Giorgini. L'Arca, Milan 1995
Vittorio Giorgini. Marco Del Francia. Angelo Pontecorboli, Florence 2000
L'architecture d'aujourd'hui № 349, November – December 2003

ANTONIO GUACCI

*1912 in Trani, †1995. Studied in Padua; graduated in 1939. Prior to establishing his own office in Trieste he worked with Umberto Nordio and, as a member of different teams, took part in competitions. In 1961, in issue № 64 of the magazine *L'architettura*, several of Guacci's projects were published, among them an expressive tower-like structure for nuns and a social housing complex, both in Trieste; in 1968, the same magazine presented the church on Monte Grisa, plus his school on Via del Boveto in Barcola, a district in Trieste. Guacci was also a sculptor; in his drawings he developed ornamental fantasy projects. His book *Disegni d'architettura* documents his studies of geometrical figures, and brings together references, for example, to Buckminster Fuller's Expo dome and to the spherical house by Ledoux. Beginning in 1945, Guacci taught in Trieste. Sergio Musmeci (*1926 in Rome, †1981 Rome) was responsible for the structural engineering of the church on Monte Grisa. Because the site is highly exposed to the elements, Musmeci made a number of experiments, including wind-tunnel tests at Turin's aeronautical institute.

- SANTUARIO DI MONTE GRISA, TRIESTE, PROSECCO, 1959–66 →**143**

SELECTED BIBLIOGRAPHY

L'architettura, cronache e storia № 151, May 1968
Disegni d'architettura di Antonio Guacci. Dino Coppo, Marco Pozzetto. Istituto di Disegno, Trieste 1987

VICO MAGISTRETTI

*1920 in Milan, †2006 in Milan. Studied architecture in Lausanne and Milan; graduated in 1945. During the early nineteen-fifties, he planned numerous social housing projects, including ten buildings for *INA-Casa*, as well as a church in Milan's Triennale district QT8 (1953–55) and an apartment tower adjacent to Parco Sempione (1953–56). His professor Ernesto N. Rogers—who, after the war, tried to establish links between rationalism and local building traditions—had a strong influence on him. In his architectural vocabulary, Magistretti—an undogmatic rationalist—also sought to achieve a balance between modernity and memory: with his design of a church in Ravello di Rescaldina (1957–59) he moved closer to neorealism, while the office building on Corso Europa (1955–57) takes cues from the International Style. At the start of the next decade, Magistretti increasingly turned his sights to furniture design and became a key figure in the development of Italian design.

- TORRE AL PARCO, MILAN, 1953–56 →**50**
- MARINA GRANDE, PINETA DI ARENZANO, 1961–65 →**194**
- HIGH-RISE APARTMENTS, MILAN, 1964–65 →**212**
- HOLIDAY HOMES, FRAMURA, 1967–70 →**244**

SELECTED BIBLIOGRAPHY

L'architettura, cronache e storia № 57, July 1960
Casabella № 284, February 1964
Lotus 1965–1966. Bruno Alfieri, Milan 1965
Domus № 432, November 1965
New Italian Architecture. Alberto Galardi. Praeger, New York 1967
Vico Magistretti. Designer. Vanni Pasca. Ernst & Sohn, Berlin 1991
Vico Magistretti. Architetto e Designer. Fulvio Irace, Vanni Pasca. Electa, Milan 1999

SELECTED WORK

Church, Milan, QT8, Piazza Santa Maria Nascente, 1953–55
Office building, Milan, Corso Europa 22, 1955–57
Church, Ravello di Rescaldina, Viale Lombardia, Via Guglielmo Marconi, 1957–59
San Felice residential district (with Luigi Caccia Dominioni), Segrate, Via San Bovio, Strada Anulare, 1967–75 [→italomodern 2, **422**]

ANGELO MANGIAROTTI

*1921 in Milan, †2012 in Milan. Studied architecture at the Politecnico in Milan; graduated in 1948. He was involved in the preparations for the 8th and 9th Milan Triennale (1948, 1951). During his stay in the United States (1953–54) he was guest professor at the IIT in Chicago and came into contact with Wright, Mies van der Rohe, Gropius, and Wachsmann. In 1955, following his return to Italy, he and Bruno Morassutti set up an office together in Milan. During the next five extremely productive years they realized important buildings such as the Glass Church in Baranzate and the apartment building on Via Quadronno, as well as furniture series, clocks, and sewing machines.
In 1961, he and Morassutti dissolved their partnership. Mangiarotti increasingly turned his attention to prefabrication—both for industrial structures (such as the production building in Cinisello Balsamo, 1968) and for dwellings (such as the apartment building in Monza, which makes use of a prefabricated wall system).
In addition to working on highly divergent architecture commissions, Mangiarotti also always engaged in industrial design and experimented with many materials and objects: from porcelain vases, chandeliers, extruded plastic profiles, and concrete lamps to his iconic marble tables. Mangiarotti taught as guest professor at universities throughout Europe, in North and South America, and in Japan.

- CHIESA MATER MISERICORDIAE (WITH BRUNO MORASSUTTI), MILAN, BARANZATE, 1956–57 →**72**
- APARTMENT BUILDING (WITH BRUNO MORASSUTTI), MILAN, 1959–62 →**136**
- APARTMENT BUILDING (WITH BRUNO MORASSUTTI), MILAN, 1960–62 →**154**
- HOLIDAY HOMES, COSTERMANO, 1971 →**298**
- APARTMENT BUILDING, MONZA, 1972 →**308**
- SNAIDERO FURNITURE FACTORY, MAJANO, 1976–78 →**314**

SELECTED BIBLIOGRAPHY

Casabella № 224, February 1959
The New Architecture of Europe. G. E. Kidder Smith. World Publishing, Cleveland 1961
Angelo Mangiarotti. Exhibition catalogue, Olivetti-Gallery, Vienna 1965
New Italian Architecture. Alberto Galardi. Praeger, New York 1967
Bauen + Wohnen № 6, June 1977

28/78 Architettura. Domus, Milan 1979
Mangiarotti. Enrico Bona. Sagep, Genoa 1988
Italian Architecture: 1945–1985. Francesco Dal Co, Sergio Polano. a+u Extra Edition, Tokyo 1988
Guida all'architettura italiana del Novecento. Sergio Polano. Electa, Milan 1991
Domus № 807, Itinerario 148: "Mangiarotti e Milano," September 1998
Milano. Giuliana Gramigna, Sergio Mazza. Ulrico Hoepli, Milan 2001
su Mangiarotti. Beppe Finessi. Abitare Segesta Cataloghi, Milan 2002
Mangiarotti. Beppe Finessi. Corraini, Mantua 2009
Angelo Mangiarotti. François Burkhardt. Motta Architettura, Milan 2010

SELECTED WORK

Pair of houses (with Bruno Morassutti), San Martino di Castrozza, Via Passo Rolle, 1954–57 [→italomodern 2, **82**]
Casa Morassutti (with Bruno Morassutti), San Martino di Castrozza, Via del Priore 24, 1957–58 [→italomodern 2, **168**]
Apartment building (with Bruno Morassutti), Milan, Via Fezzan, 1958
Casa Fontanesi, Marina di Pietrasanta, Via Cortona 146, 1967–68 [→italomodern 2, **386**]
Armitalia factory, Cinisello Balsamo, Via Pelizza da Volpedo 109, 1968
Apartment building, Arosio, Via Marconi 17, 1977
Unifor furniture factory, Turate, Via Isonzo 1, 1982

GIOVANNI MICHELUCCI

*1891 in Pistoia, †1990 in Fiesole. Studied architecture in Pistoia and Florence; graduated in 1914. Taught from 1920 to 1928 in Rome and then in Florence and Bologna until his retirement in 1966. He began his long career with classicist villas in Pistoia and Rome, and then, as a member of the *Gruppo Toscano*, created an important work of *Razionalismo*: Florence's Central Station (1932–35). Shortly after the war he built Pistoia's stock exchange: it became a classic example of inserting a new building in a historical setting. From 1957 to 1965, he converted that very stock exchange to a bank headquarters. In his design for an apartment tower in Livorno (1956–66) he experimented with irregular forms and the seemingly random arrangement of verandas and balconies. His later work is characterized by dynamic spatial concepts and forms (recorded with pencil and brush on paper and in numerous buildings) and increasing dedication to the design of churches.

- CHIESA DEL CUORE IMMACOLATO DI MARIA, PISTOIA, 1959–61 →**130**
- CHIESA DELL'IMMACOLATA CONCEZIONE DI MARIA VERGINE, LONGARONE, 1966–78 →**232**
- PARSONAGE, ARZIGNANO, 1968–81 →**274**

SELECTED BIBLIOGRAPHY

Giovanni Michelucci. RIBA Exhibiton, London. Modulo, Florence 1978
Giovanni Michelucci. Amedeo Belluzzi, Claudia Conforti. Electa, Milan 1986
Perspecta № 27, Yale Architectural Journal, New Haven 1992
Giovanni Michelucci. Gianni Biondillo. Testo & Immagine, Turin 1999

SELECTED WORK

Stazione di Santa Maria Novella (with *Gruppo Toscano*), Florence, Piazza della Stazione, 1932–35
Bank, Pistoia, Via San Matteo 5, 1957–65
High-rise apartments, Livorno, Piazza Giacomo Matteotti 2, 1956–66
Chiesa dell'Autostrada, Campi Bisenzio, Via di Limite, 1960–64
Santuario della Beata Vergine della Consolazione, San Marino, Borgo Maggiore, Via XXVIII Luglio, 1961–67 [→italomodern 2, **254**]
Bank (with Bruno Sacchi), Colle di Val d'Elsa, Via di Spugna 2, 1973–83 [→italomodern 2, **518**]

GIULIO MINOLETTI

∗1910 in Milan, †1981 in Milan. Studied architecture at the Politecnico in Milan; graduated in 1931. He returned there to teach from 1933 to 1948. In addition to architecture, he engaged in city planning and industrial design. For example, he designed the streamlined Breda trains, as well as the interiors of transatlantic ocean liners (*Africa*, *Andrea Doria*, *Cristoforo Colombo* and *Leonardo da Vinci*, 1952–59), and a passenger aircraft (Breda-Zappata). He also found acclaim as author of numerous essays on architecture and city planning. As Giò Ponti put it, Minoletti was an architect of "typical Italian versatility."

• APARTMENT BUILDING, MILAN, 1957–59 →**106**

SELECTED BIBLIOGRAPHY

Minoletti. Edizioni Milano Moderna, Milan 1959
L'architettura, cronache e storia № 96, October 1963
New Italian Architecture. Alberto Galardi. Praeger, New York 1967
Domus № 774, Itinerario 115: "Minoletti e Milano," September 1995
Minoletti – Carrà. Gianfranco Farioli. Electa, Milan 2009

SELECTED WORK

Holiday home on Lake Como, Fiumelatte, Strada Provinciale, 1940
Apartment building, Milan, QT8, Via Pogatschnig 32, 1950–51
Swimming pool, Sporting Club Brianza, Monza, Viale Brianza 39, 1951
Mixed-use building, Milan, Via Cernaia 2, Via Fatebenefratelli 3, 1951–57
Department store, Milan, Corso San Gottardo 29, 1959–65

RICCARDO MORANDI

∗1902 in Rome, †1989 in Rome. Studied engineering in Rome; graduated in 1927. Morandi produced a large oeuvre including several movie theaters and apartment buildings, the reinforced concrete church in Colleferro (1934–36) and, beginning in 1945, numerous bridges, large halls, and factory structures. Of particular note is his early involvement with pre-tensioned concrete structures: in 1948 he patented his pre-tensioning method, *Sistema Morandi*. From 1950 onward, as a specialist for bridge engineering he was active around the globe—in Venezuela, as well as in South Africa, Canada, Ecuador, Libya, and Colombia. Morandi taught at the architecture faculty in Florence from 1959 to 1969 and was professor of bridge construction at the engineering faculty in Rome from 1969 to 1972.

• HIGHWAY BRIDGE, GENOA, 1960–67 →**170**

SELECTED BIBLIOGRAPHY

L'architettura, cronache e storia № 120, October 1965
28/78 Architettura. Domus, Milan 1979
Casabella № 469, May 1981
Modern Architecture. Manfredo Tafuri, Francesco Dal Co. Rizzoli, New York 1986
Italian Architecture: 1945–1985. Francesco Dal Co, Sergio Polano. a+u Extra Edition, Tokyo 1988
Riccardo Morandi. Gangemi, Rome 1991
Guida all'architettura italiana del Novecento. Sergio Polano. Electa, Milan 1991
L'architettura del Novecento. Cesare de'Seta. Garzanti, Milan 1992
Genova. Guide to modern architecture. Alinea, Florence 2004
Genoa. 100 Years of Architecture. De Ferrari, Genoa 2004

SELECTED WORK

Maracaibo Bridge, Venezuela, 1957–62
Exhibition hall for the Turin Motor Show, Turin, Corso Massimo d'Azeglio 15, 1958–59 [→italomodern 2, **198**]
Hangars at Fiumicino Airport, Rome, 1961 and 1969–70
Wadi el Kuf Bridge, Libya, 1965–71
Office building (with Oscar Niemeyer), Pianezza, Via Piave, Via dei Prati, 1976–79

BRUNO MORASSUTTI

*1920 in Padua, †2008 in Belluno. Studied architecture in Venice; graduated in 1947. Internship at Taliesin East and Taliesin West from 1949 to 1950. The house for two families in Jesolo (1950–54), his first project following his return from America, reveals the profound influence Frank Lloyd Wright had on him. This applies to the Romanelli Residence in Udine, as well, which was begun by Angelo Masieri in 1952 and completed four years later by Morassutti and Carlo Scarpa. In 1955, Morassutti and Angelo Mangiarotti set up an architecture practice together in Milan. In just a few years' time they realized a number of important buildings—for instance, the Glass Church in Baranzate, the holiday homes in San Martino di Castrozza and the apartment building on Via Gavirate in Milan—and several icons of industrial design. In the early sixties, the two architects established separate offices. Morassutti went on to design holiday flats in San Martino di Castrozza (1963–66), a generously dimensioned apartment building in Padua (1966), and the training center in Novedrate (1970–74).

- CHIESA MATER MISERICORDIAE (WITH ANGELO MANGIAROTTI), MILAN, BARANZATE, 1956–57 →**72**
- APARTMENT BUILDUNG (WITH ANGELO MANGIAROTTI), MILAN, 1959–62 →**136**
- APARTMENT BUILDUNG (WITH ANGELO MANGIAROTTI), MILAN, 1960–62 →**154**
- IBM TRAINING CENTER, NOVEDRATE, 1970–74 →**284**

SELECTED BIBLIOGRAPHY

Casabella № 224, February 1959
The New Architecture of Europe. G. E. Kidder Smith. World Publishing, Cleveland 1961
New Italian Architecture. Alberto Galardi. Praeger, New York 1967
Bruno Morassutti. 1920–2008 opere e progetti. Electa, Milan 2009

SELECTED WORK

Casa Morassutti (with Angelo Mangiarotti), San Martino di Castrozza, Via del Priore 24, 1957–58 [→italomodern 2, **168**]
Condominio Le Fontanelle, San Martino di Castrozza, Via Bartolo Zagonel, 1963–66 [→italomodern 2, **308**]
Apartment building, Padua, Via Falloppio 39, 1966 [→italomodern 2, **372**]

LUIGI MORETTI

*1907 in Rome, †1973 in Capraia. Studied architecture in Rome. Set up his office while still a student; completed his thesis in 1930. Beginning in 1933, Moretti received numerous commissions for public buildings, such as the fencing academy at the Mussolini Forum (1933–36) and buildings for fascist youth organizations in Piacenza (1933–34), Rome (1933–37) and Trecate (1934–36). After the war, he and Adolfo Fossatoro founded *Cofimprese*, a construction-financing society, and in that capacity Moretti became the client for his own important projects, among them the iconic *Il Girasole* apartment building in Rome (1947–50) and the mixed-use building on Corso Italia in Milan. In the mid-fifties, Moretti's formal vocabulary evolved from the ambivalent modernism of *Il Girasole* toward an expressive, neo-baroque modernism. This is exemplified by *La Saracena*, a holiday home in Santa Marinella (1954–57), the Watergate complex in Washington (1960–65) and the thermal baths of Fiuggi (1964–72). Moretti founded and headed *Spazio*, an art and architecture journal; between 1950 and 1953, a total of seven editions appeared.

- MIXED-USE BUILDING, MILAN, 1949–56 →**30**

SELECTED BIBLIOGRAPHY

Luigi Moretti. Salvatore Santuccio. Zanichelli, Bologna 1986
Luigi Moretti. Works and Writings. Princeton Architectural Press, New York 2002

SELECTED WORK

Fencing academy, Rome, Foro Italico, Via dei Gladiatori, 1933–36
Il Girasole, Rome, Viale Bruno Buozzi 64, 1947–50
Villa La Saracena, Santa Marinella, Lungomare Guglielmo Marconi 135, 1954–57
Watergate complex, Washington D.C., New Hampshire Avenue NW, 1960–65
Stock Exchange Tower (with Pier Luigi Nervi), Montreal, Place Victoria, 1960–65
Health spa, Fiuggi, Piazzale Lucarelli d'Anticoli, 1964–72

GIOVANNI MUZIO

∗1893 in Milan, † 1982 in Milan. Studied architecture at the Politecnico in Milan; graduated in 1915. Established an office with Mino Fiocchi, Emilio Lancia, Giuseppe de Finetti and Giò Ponti in 1920. Muzio spearheaded the group known as *Novecento Milanese*, and with his design of the Ca'Brütta (1919–22)—in the Lombard dialect, "the ugly house"—he created the movement's manifesto. His formal vocabulary fluctuated between tradition, classicist rigor and rationality. In his Palazzo dell'Arte (1932–33), the Triennale's exhibition hall, pared-down classicism merges with a utilitarian brick structure. He employed brick in many of his buildings, for example, in an eleven-story apartment building on Piazza della Repubblica (1935–36) and a church on Milan's periphery (1956–58). Muzio taught at the Politecnico in Milan and at the Politecnico in Turin.

- TORRE TURATI, MILAN, 1966–69 →**230**

SELECTED BIBLIOGRAPHY

Casabella № 342, November 1969
Casabella № 440/441, October – November 1978
Muzio. L'architettura di Giovanni Muzio. Abitare Segesta, Milan 1994
Milano. Giuliana Gramigna, Sergio Mazza. Ulrico Hoepli, Milan 2001

SELECTED WORK

Ca'Brütta, Milan, Via Moscova 12–14, Via Turati, 1919–22
La Triennale, Palazzo dell'Arte, Milan, Via Alemagna 6, Parco Sempione, 1932–33
Villa Leidi, Bergamo, Viale Vittorio Emanuele 78, 1935
Apartment building, Milan, Piazza della Repubblica 5–9, 1935–36
Angelicum convent, Milan, Piazza Sant'Angelo 2, Via Renzo Bertoni, 1939–40
Church, Milan, Piazza San Giovanni Battista alla Creta 11, 1956–58

PIER LUIGI NERVI

∗1891 in Sondrio, † 1979 in Rome. Studied civil engineering in Bologna; graduated in 1913. Ten years later he founded his office in Rome. Nervi designed Florence's soccer stadium from 1930 to 1932 and, after that, several hangars. As both designer and engineer he developed a variety of lightweight lattice structures employing prefabricated concrete elements. The vault of the exhibition hall in Turin (1947–48), consisting of wave-shaped, prefabricated elements, spans ninety-five meters. In the late forties, he experimented with ultra-thin concrete shells and invented "ferrocement." Nervi published a comprehensive series of books on the history of world architecture and taught structural engineering at the architecture faculty at La Sapienza in Rome.

- BOATYARD (WITH LUIGI CARLO DANERI), SAN MICHELE DI PAGANA, 1948–50 →**14**
- PAPER FACTORY, MANTUA, 1960–64 →**168**

SELECTED BIBLIOGRAPHY

Italy Builds. G. E. Kidder Smith. The Architectural Press, London 1955
Pier Luigi Nervi. Bauten und Projekte. Verlag Gerd Hatje, Stuttgart 1957
Pier Luigi Nervi. Ada Louise Huxtable. George Braziller, New York 1960
P. L. Nervi. Neue Strukturen. Gerd Hatje, Stuttgart 1963
Architectural Forum July 1964
Costruire correttamente. Pier Luigi Nervi. Hoepli, Milan 1965
Pier Luigi Nervi. Serie di Architettura 5. Zanichelli, Bologna 1979
Modernità dell'architettura nel territorio mantovano. Tre Lune, Mantua 2003

SELECTED WORK

Exhibition hall, Turin, Corso Massimo d'Azeglio, 1947–48
Tobacco warehouse, Bologna, Via Ferrarese, 1951–52
Torre Pirelli (with Giò Ponti), Milan, Piazza Duca d'Aosta 3, 1955–61
Palazzetto dello Sport, Rome, Piazza Apollodoro, 1956–58
Palazzo del Lavoro (with Antonio Nervi, Gino Covre), Turin, Via Ventimiglia 211, 1959–61 [→italomodern 2, **222**]

GABRIELLA PADOVANO, CESARE BLASI, UGO LA PIETRA, ALBERTO SEASSARO

The four architects and designers did not form an official team, but repeatedly joined forces in different constellations. In this manner, Seassaro and La Pietra developed projects in the art and design milieu, and Padovano and Blasi built a housing complex on Via Airolo (1971). The Politecnico in Milan—where all four taught—and the strong influence of Vittoriano Viganò constitute common denominators. In 1961, Cesare Blasi teamed up with Luigi Figini and Gino Pollini for the design of the hotel and residence on Largo Augusto in Milan. Two years later, Blasi wrote a monograph on Figini and Pollini, two grand masters of *Razionalismo*.

- HOUSING COMPLEX, 1973–78 →**310**

SELECTED BIBLIOGRAPHY

L'architettura, cronache e storia № 271, May 1978
Milano. Maurizio Grandi, Attilio Pracchi. Zanichelli, Bologna 1980
Guida all'architettura italiana del Novecento. Sergio Polano. Electa, Milan 1991

SELECTED WORK

Housing complex, Milan, Via Airolo 36–44, 1971

LUIGI PELLEGRIN

∗1925 in Courcelette, France, †2001 in Rome. Studied architecture in Rome; graduated in 1948. Pellegrin was a member of Bruno Zevi's *Organic Architecture* movement. In his early work the direct influence of Frank Lloyd Wright can be discerned, especially in the post offices in Saronno and Suzzara (both 1958). After building several housing complexes and the apartment tower in Giulianova (1962) he turned his attention primarily to the construction of schools; his oeuvre comprises some 200 of them. Pellegrin planned a prefabricated, standardized school for Saudi Arabia (1975–77)—the design was then implemented in many other settings—as well as the International School in Riad (1975). He also realized buildings in Venezuela, Nigeria, Chad, Spain, and Senegal.

- ISTITUTO PER GEOMETRI E LICEO SCIENTIFICO, PISA, 1971–76 →**306**

SELECTED BIBLIOGRAPHY

L'architettura, cronache e storia № 300, October 1980
Guida all'architettura italiana del Novecento. Sergio Polano. Electa, Milan 1991
Luigi Pellegrin. Il mestiere di Architetto. Prospettive Edizioni, Rome 2001
Luigi Pellegrin. Silvana, Milan 2003

SELECTED WORK

Post office, Saronno, Via Alessandro Manzoni, 1958
Post office, Suzzara, Via Giuseppe Mazzini, 1958
Housing complex, Gaeta, Via della Breccia, 1962
High-rise apartments, Giulianova Lido, Via Foscolo, 1962
Istituto Tecnico per Geometri, Vicenza, Viale Astichello 195, 1970–74

GIUSEPPE (PINO) PIZZIGONI

∗1901 in Bergamo, † 1967 in Bergamo. Studied architecture at the Politecnico in Milan; graduated in 1925. Early projects with Giovanni Muzio. The design of his first building, a house for his father (1925–27), was influenced by *Novecento Milanese*, a neoclassicist movement. His own house, Casa Cubo (1936–37), in contrast, was a pared-down building with pilotis and flat roof. In 1949, Pizzigoni headed the organization committee for the CIAM Congress in Bergamo (CIAM VII, Art and Architecture). His late work was characterized by experimentation with thin concrete shells.

- CASA MINIMA, BERGAMO, 1946 →**10**
- CHIESA SANTA MARIA IMMACOLATA, BERGAMO, 1960–63 →**162**

SELECTED BIBLIOGRAPHY

Pizzigoni. Invito allo spazio, progetti e architetture. 1923–1967. Electa, Milan, 1982

Domus № 801, Itinerario 142: "Pizzigoni e Bergamo," February 1998

SELECTED WORK

House for the architect's father, Bergamo, Viale Vittorio Emanuele II 70, 1925–27

Casa Cubo, Bergamo, Via Monte Ortigara 35, 1936–37

Family tomb, Bergamo, Cimitero Civico, 1947

Additions to the Donizetti Theater, Bergamo, Piazza Cavour 14, 1959–64

Pigsty, Torre Pallavicina, Via Sante Giulie 50, 1960–64 [→italomodern 2, **234**]

City hall, Zandobbio, Piazza Monumento, 1962–65 [→italomodern 2, **272**]

Casa Nani, Parre, Via Sant'Alberto, 1964–65 [→italomodern 2, **320**]

GIÒ PONTI

∗1891 in Milan, † 1979 in Milan. Studied architecture at the Politecnico in Milan; graduated in 1921. During the nineteen-twenties, Ponti was involved in *Novecento Milanese*, a neoclassicist movement spearheaded by Giovanni Muzio. Ponti joined forces with Emilio Lancia to realize several buildings, for example, the apartment building on Piazza Amendola (1928–30). In the mid-thirties Ponti turned toward rationalism. This phase yielded projects such as Torre Littoria (1932–33), the literature faculty at the university in Padua (1934–38) and the Montecatini office building in Milan (1935–38). With his design of the Pirelli skyscraper in Milan (1956–61) Ponti created an urban landmark, and his Superleggera chair (1957) is an icon of Italian furniture design. Ponti's oeuvre comprises residential districts as well as extravagant houses, such as Villa Planchart in Venezuela (1954–55). He also designed churches, hotels and interiors of boats, as well as serially manufactured products, from coffee machines and lamps to glazed ceramic tiles. Giò Ponti founded and headed the magazines *Domus* (1928–41 and 1948–79) and *Stile* (1941–47). He taught at the Politecnico in Milan from 1936 to 1961.

- CHIESA SAN FRANCESCO AL FOPPONINO, MILAN, 1961–64 →**190**
- CASA SOTTO UNA FOGLIA (WITH NANDA VIGO), MALO, 1964–69 →**216**

SELECTED BIBLIOGRAPHY

Domus № 414, May 1964

Domus № 482, January 1970

Giò Ponti. Ceramica e architettura. Centro Di, Florence 1987

Giò Ponti. The Complete Work 1923–1978. MIT Press, Cambridge 1990

L'albero di Giò Ponti. Alberto Bassi. Museo Casabianca, Malo 2003

SELECTED WORK

Apartment building, Milan, Piazza Amendola, Via Domenichino 1, 1928–30

Torre Littoria, Milan, Parco Sempione, Via Alemagna, 1932–33

Faculty building, Padua, Piazza Capitaniato, 1934–38

Palazzo Montecatini, Milan, Via Moscova 3, 1935–38

Torre Pirelli (with Pier Luigi Nervi), Milan, Piazza Duca d'Aosta, 1956–61

GIORGIO RAINERI

*1927 in Turin, †2012. Studied architecture in Turin; graduated in 1949. During the early nineteen-fifties Raineri and Roberto Gabetti built several *INA-Casa* housing complexes. Aimaro Isola then joined the team for the stock exchange of Turin (1952–56). In Raineri's own practice, Catholic organizations were among his most important clients: beginning with the school on Via Monfalcone (1957–58)—a spare and finely detailed brick building—and progressing to the novitiate in Valsalice (1962–66), with a memorable roof landscape, and the adjacent retirement home known as Casa Rotonda (1968–72) to the designs for altars in his late oeuvre. Like the farm in Montalenghe, Raineri's single-family homes are characterized by striking roof forms and the uniform materiality of brick walls and roofs.

- OLIVETTI FARM, MONTALENGHE, 1957–58 →**100**
- CASA-ALBERGO ECA (WITH GABETTI & ISOLA), TURIN, 1964–68 →**214**

SELECTED BIBLIOGRAPHY

Casabella № 227, May 1959
L'architettura, cronache e storia № 152, June 1968
Giorgio Raineri Architetto. Tamara Del Bel Belluz. Celid, Turin 1988
Architetture olivettiane a Ivrea. Gangemi, Rome 1988
Olivetti Builds. Modern Architecture in Ivrea. Patrizia Bonifazio, Paolo Scrivano. Skira, Milan 2001

SELECTED WORK

School, Turin, Via Monfalcone 28, 1957–58
Novitiate, Turin, Valsalice, Via Principessa Felicita di Savoia 14, 1962–66
Apartment building and preschool, Turin, Corso Unione Sovietica 223, 1965–68
Casa Rotonda, Turin, Valsalice, Viale Enrico Thovez 43, 1968–72
Preschool (with Lorenzo Mamino), Mondovì, Corso Europa 24, 1969–70 [→italomodern 2, **452**]

LEONARDO RICCI

*1918 in Rome, †1994 in Venice. Studied architecture in Florence; graduated in 1942. Ricci subsequently became assistant professor under Giovanni Michelucci at the same university and worked in his office until 1946. Ricci's first important project, the flower market in Pescia (1948–51), came about in cooperation with Leonardo Savioli. The design received several prizes and established both architects' reputations as protagonists of the Tuscan School. Beginning in 1949, Ricci built the Villaggio di Monterinaldi, a collection of houses in the hills outside Florence; he also built himself a residence and studio there. Like in the holiday home (1957–59) he planned for Elisabeth Mann Borgese (the daughter of Thomas Mann), stone walls play a decisive role. His introspective book *Anonymous*, which appeared in 1962, was translated to English by Mann Borgese. Ricci taught in Florence and was guest professor at MIT.

- OFFICE BUILDING (WITH EZIO BIENAIMÈ, ALDO PISANI), MASSA, 1960 →**148**

SELECTED BIBLIOGRAPHY

Leonardo Ricci. Anonymous (20th Century). George Braziller, New York 1962
Itinerari Apuani di Architettura Moderna. Alinea, Florence 1989
Leonardo Ricci. Giovanni Bartolozzi. Testo & Immagine, Turin 2004

SELECTED WORK

Flower market (with Leonardo Savioli), Pescia, Via Amendola, Via Turati, 1948–51
Casa Ricci, Florence, Via di Monterinaldi 21, 1949–64 [→italomodern 2, **20**]
Casa Mann Borgese, Forte dei Marmi, Via Thomas Mann 3, 1957–58
Casa Balmain, Elba, Poggio, Via della Fontanella, 1958–59
Sorgane residential district (with Leonardo Savioli), Florence, Via Isonzo, Via Tagliamento, 1962–80 [→italomodern 2, **278**]

RIDOLFI & FRANKL

MARIO RIDOLFI
∗1904 in Rome, †1984 in Marmore. Studied architecture in Rome; graduated in 1929. Took part in the first exhibitions hosted by *MIAR* (*Movimento Italiano per l'Architettura Razionale*). Ridolfi was initially considered an adherent of rationalism and received commissions for important buildings such as the post office on Piazza Bologna in Rome (1932–35). After the war, he was at the forefront of another movement, *Neorealismo*: the Quartiere Tiburtino in Rome (1949–55) is a built manifesto of it.

WOLFGANG (VOLFANGO) FRANKL
∗1907 in Munich, †1994 in Terni. Studied architecture in Stuttgart; graduated in 1932 and then moved to Rome. Ridolfi and Frankl set up a practice together in 1933. The war interrupted their work—Frankl emigrated to England—but it resumed in 1948. Their large oeuvre includes residential districts in all of Italy. Beginning in the sixties, most of their commissions were in the province of Terni. Consequently, in 1970, they relocated their office from Rome to Marmore. Their late work consists primarily of private residences with stone walls and complex floor plans.

- OLIVETTI PRESCHOOL, IVREA, 1954–68 →**64**
- VILLAGGIO COORDINATO, TREVISO, 1956–63 →**82**

SELECTED BIBLIOGRAPHY

Casabella № 221, September–October 1958
Casabella № 249, March 1961
L'architettura, cronache e storia № 133, November 1966
Bauen + Wohnen № 2/3, February – March 1977
Mario Ridolfi. Fabrizio Brunetti. Alinea, Florence 1987
Mario Ridolfi. Guida all'architettura. Valerio Palmieri. Arsenale, Venice 1997

SELECTED WORK
Post office, Rome, Piazza Bologna, 1932–35
Quartiere Tiburtino, Rome, Via Tiburtina, Via Diego Angeli, 1949–55
Housing complex, Rome, Viale Etiopia, Via Tripolitania 195–211, 1949–56
Casa Lina, Marmore, Via Casa Lina, 1964–67

ALDO ROSSI

∗1931 in Milan, †1997 in Milan. Studied architecture at the Politecnico in Milan; graduated in 1959. While still a student, he worked for Ignazio Gardella and Marco Zanuso. Beginning in 1955, he wrote articles for *Casabella*. Rossi was an editor at the magazine until 1964, when Ernesto Rogers stepped down as editor-in-chief. In 1963, he began to teach at different universities, but on account of his political and cultural activities, he was banned from teaching in Italy for four years. That prompted a highly acclaimed stint as guest professor at the ETH Zurich before he was appointed professor at the IUAV in Venice in 1975. Rossi's first realization—the holiday home in Marina di Massa—was still clearly influenced by Adolf Loos, but by 1965 his characteristic formal vocabulary had already crystalized in his design of the partisan monument in Segrate. One year later, he published his manifesto *L'architettura della città* (the English edition, entitled *The Architecture of the City*, appeared in 1982). In his drawings and collages Rossi made countless studies of archetypical themes.

- HOLIDAY HOME, MARINA DI MASSA, 1960 →**146**
- GALLARATESE HOUSING COMPLEX (WITH CARLO AYMONINO), MILAN, 1967–74 →**250**

SELECTED BIBLIOGRAPHY

Casabella № 291, September 1964
Lotus international № 7, 1970
Aldo Rossi. Projects and drawings 1962–1979. Centro Di, Florence 1979
GA Document. Special Issue 1970–1980, Tokyo 1980
Aldo Rossi. Gianni Braghieri. Zanichelli, Bologna 1981
Modern Architecture. Manfredo Tafuri, Francesco Dal Co. Rizzoli, New York 1986
Itinerari Apuani di Architettura Moderna. Pietro Giorgieri. Alinea, Florence 1989

SELECTED WORK
Monument to the Partisans of World War II, Segrate, Via 25 Aprile, 1965
San Sabba School (with Renzo Agosto, Giorgio Grassi, Francesco Tentori), Trieste, Salita di Zugnano 5, 1968–69 [→italomodern 2, **432**]
Cemetery, Modena, Strada Cimitero San Cataldo, 1971–83
Housing cooperative, Goito, Strada Pedagno, Viale San Giovanni Bosco, 1979

GIUSEPPE SAMONÀ

*1898 in Palermo, †1983 in Rome. Studied civil engineering in Palermo; graduated in 1922. Taught in Naples from 1931 to 1936 and then in Venice. Under his direction the architecture school in Venice became a leading institution. In 1930, Samonà won the competition for the reconstruction of the Palazzata—Messina's imposing harbor promenade, which comprises several buildings—and there he built the Palazzo Littorio (1936–40) and four additional elongated buildings (through 1958). For a site across from Venice's Central Station and next to San Simeon Piccolo, he planned an office building (1952–56) with a facade whose slender reinforced concrete columns and stucco pilasters interact three-dimensionally. Beginning in 1974, Samonà and his son Alberto (*1932 in Naples, †1993 in Rome) prepared designs for a new theater for the city of Sciacca. It is made up of elementary shapes—a truncated cone, a prism and a truncated pyramid—and, like a raw concrete sculpture, stands on the southern coast of Sicily. Construction began in 1979. Three years later, the project—though near completion—was scrapped.

- MIXED-USE BUILDING, TREVISO, 1949–53 →**26**

SELECTED BIBLIOGRAPHY

Italian Architecture: 1945–1985. Francesco Dal Co, Sergio Polano. a+u Extra Edition, Tokyo 1988
Guida all'architettura italiana del Novecento. Sergio Polano. Electa, Milan 1991
Giuseppe e Alberto Samonà. Francesco Tentori. Testo & Immagine, Turin 1996
Novecento. Edilizia Moderna a Treviso. Alfonso Cendron. Vianello Libri, Treviso 2001

SELECTED WORK

Palazzata, Messina, Via Vittorio Emanuele II, 1930–58
Residential district, Mestre, Viale San Marco, Via Antonio Lamberti, 1951–56
Office building, Venice, Campiello della Comare, 1952–56
Theater (with Alberto Samonà), Sciacca, Piazza delle Terme, 1974–83

LEONARDO SAVIOLI

*1917 in Florence, †1982 in Florence. Studied with Michelucci in Florence; graduated in 1941. He stayed on as assistant professor and, beginning in 1951, full professor of urban planning. In 1948, Savioli (with a team including Leonardo Ricci) won the competition for the flower market in Pescia, a shell structure open on all sides; the project aroused considerable attention and received a prize at the Biennale of São Paulo. Savioli was an important protagonist of the Tuscan School. In his residential projects of the fifties he experimented with projecting roofs and staggered levels. The next decade saw him turn his attention to three-dimensionally shaping individual components, for example, at Casa Taddei (1964–65). From 1962 to 1963, Savioli worked on the design of the Le Corbusier exhibition shown at Florence's Palazzo Strozzi.

- VILLAGGIO BELVEDERE HOUSING COMPLEX, PISTOIA, 1957–59 →**108**

SELECTED BIBLIOGRAPHY

Leonardo Savioli. Grafico e architetto. Centro Di, Florence 1982
Architetture per la nuova città. Alberto Donti. Alinea, Florence 1992

SELECTED WORK

Flower market (with Leonardo Ricci), Pescia, Via Amendola, Via Turati, 1948–51
Sorgane residential district (with Leonardo Ricci), Florence, Via Isonzo, Via Tagliamento, 1962–80 [→italomodern 2, **278**]
Casa Taddei, Fiesole, Via delle Fontanelle 23, 1964–65
Apartment building, Florence, Via Piagentina 29, 1964–67

GINO VALLE

*1923 in Udine, †2003 in Udine. Studied architecture in Venice; graduated in 1948 and then worked with his father Provino. In 1951, he received a Fulbright scholarship to Harvard's Graduate School of Design. From the beginning, Valle's commissions covered a vast spectrum spanning from simple residences to apartment towers (for example, in Trieste, 1955–57), and from banks, city halls and schools to industrial structures (his work with Zanussi, a manufacturer of household appliances, began in 1956). On top of all that, he designed a monument to the resistance movement in Udine (1959–69) and Pier Paolo Pasolini's grave in Casarsa (1977). Valle taught at various universities in Europe, South Africa, USA, and, from 1972 to 2001, at the IUAV in Venice. He was a member of Salzburg's design review board from 1983 to 1985.

- ZANUSSI OFFICE BUILDING, PORCIA, 1959–61 →**134**
- RESIDENCE, UDINE, 1963–66 →**210**
- CASA ROSSA, UDINE, 1965–66 →**222**
- APARTMENT BLOCK, UDINE, 1976–79 →**324**

SELECTED BIBLIOGRAPHY

Domus № 446, January 1967
ac № 45, January 1967
New Italian Architecture. Alberto Galardi. Praeger, New York 1967
New Directions in Italian Architecture. Vittorio Gregotti. George Braziller, New York 1968
Werk, Bauen + Wohnen № 7/8, July 1983
Gino Valle. Pierre-Alain Croset. Electa, Milan 1989
Gino Valle a Udine. Pierre-Alain Croset. Mazzotta, Milan 2007

SELECTED WORK

High-rise apartments, Trieste, Via San Francesco 12–14, 1955–57
Monument to the Resistence, Udine, Piazzale XXVI Luglio, 1959–69
Mixed-use building, Udine, Via Mercatovecchio 26, 1963–65
Fantoni furniture factory, Osoppo, Via Europa Unita, 1972–96
Pier Paolo Pasolini's grave, Casarsa, 1977
Housing complex, Venice, Giudecca, Calle dei Lavraneri, 1980–86

VITTORIANO VIGANÒ

*1919 in Milan, †1996 in Milan. Studied architecture at the Politecnico in Milan; graduated in 1944 and stayed on as assistant professor under Giò Ponti. In 1963, he was named full professor. In his diverse oeuvre—from the design of furniture, lamps, shops, exhibitions, and plazas to factory facilities—two projects outshine all the others: the Istituto Marchiondi boarding school in Milan and the holiday home for André Bloc in Portese. The rawness and strength of the two buildings inspire awe to this day—though the dormitory is in a state of disrepair. In Reyner Banham's classic book on brutalism he called Istituto Marchiondi one of the biggest surprises in European architecture of the late fifties.

- ISTITUTO MARCHIONDI, MILAN, 1953–59 →**52**
- HOLIDAY HOME, PORTESE, 1957–60 →**110**

SELECTED BIBLIOGRAPHY

Ville in Italia. Roberto Aloi. Ulrico Hoepli, Milan 1960
The New Architecture of Europe. G. E. Kidder Smith. World Publishing, Cleveland 1961
The New Brutalism. Reyner Banham. Karl Krämer, Stuttgart 1966
New Italian Architecture. Alberto Galardi. Praeger, New York 1967
New Directions in Italian Architecture. Vittorio Gregotti. George Braziller, New York 1968
L'architettura, cronache e storia № 166, August 1969
Twentieth Century Architecture. Dennis Sharp. Heinemann/Secker & Warburg, London 1972
Das Ende der Zuversicht. Wolfgang Pehnt. Siedler, Berlin 1983
Itinerari d'Architettura Contemporanea sul Garda. Alinea, Florence 1996
L'Istituto Marchiondi Spagliardi di Vittoriano Viganò. Mendrisio Academy Press, Mendrisio 2009

SELECTED WORK

Apartment building, Milan, Viale Piave 20, 1947–51
Apartment building, Milan, Piazza Giovanni Perego 7, 1958–59
Mollificio Bresciano factory, San Felice del Benaco, Via Umberto Zerneri, 1970–81

...NDA VIGO

...36 in Milan. Studied architecture in Lausanne. ...960, she set up her design studio in Milan and ...sed extravagant interiors, luminaires, spatial ...llations, and furniture. Consequently, her work ...d be seen both in art exhibitions and at the ...nale of Milan design shows. Beginning in 1967, ... designed a museum for art collector Remo ...disi; the building also served as his residence. ...s center is a large cylindrical void, around which ...ooms of the three main levels are organized. ...the house in Malo, all floors and walls are ...red in white tile.

...SA SOTTO UNA FOGLIA (WITH GIÒ PONTI), ...ALO, 1964–69 →**216**

...CTED BIBLIOGRAPHY

...us № 414, May 1964
...l Interior, "Southern Europe." Tokyo 1972
...us № 482, January 1970
...ro di Giò Ponti. Alberto Bassi. Museo ...sabianca, Malo 2003
...a Vigo. Barbara Pastor. Abitare Segesta, ...ilan 2006

...LECTED WORK

...sa Museo Remo Brindisi, Lido di Spina, Via Nicolò Pisano 45, 1967–71 [→italomodern 2, **402**]

MARCO ZANUSO

*1916 in Milan, †2001 in Milan. Studied architecture at the Politecnico in Milan; graduated in 1939. Set up his office in 1945. From the beginning he worked both as architect and as designer. He designed numerous residential buildings, holiday homes, factory facilities, and cultural buildings, but also furniture, radios, television sets, telephones, and clocks. In addition, he was an editor both at *Domus* and at *Casabella*, as well as co-founder of a society for industrial design. Zanuso taught from 1961 to 1991 at the Politecnico in Milan. His large oeuvre contains an anomaly: a folly—a fairy-tale whale in the form of an open concrete dome (1962)—for the Pinocchio theme park in Collodi.

• APARTMENT BUILDINGS, MILAN, 1961–64 →**186**

SELECTED BIBLIOGRAPHY

L'architettura, cronache e storia № 123, January 1966
28/78 Architettura. Domus, Milan 1979
Milano. Maurizio Grandi, Attilio Pracchi. Zanichelli, Bologna 1980
Il Condominio a Milano. Di Baio, Milan 1987
Italian Architecture: 1945–1985. Francesco Dal Co, Sergio Polano. a+u Extra Edition, Tokyo 1988
Marco Zanuso Architetto. Manolo De Giorgi. Skira, Milan 1999
Milano. Giuliana Gramigna, Sergio Mazza. Ulrico Hoepli, Milan 2001

SELECTED WORK

Olivetti factory, Buenos Aires, Merlo, Gral. Paz, 1954–61
Olivetti factory, São Paulo, Rua Camilo Olivetti, 1956–61
Residence, Milan, Via 20 Settembre 5, 1960–64
Folly, Collodi, Parco di Pinocchio, Via di San Gennaro 3, 1962
Brionvega factory, Casella d'Asolo, Viale Enrico Fermi, 1963–67
Olivetti factory, Scarmagno, Strada di Montalenghe 8, 1967–70
Case popolari, Genoa, Pra', Via della Benedicta, 1976 [→italomodern 2, **532**]

Z

CONCEPT
Martin Feiersinger, Werner Feiersinger,
Arno Ritter, Willi Schmid

PHOTOGRAPHS
Werner Feiersinger, Martin Feiersinger

ESSAY
Otto Kapfinger

PROJECT SUMMARIES
Martin Feiersinger with Michaela Zöschg
and Christian Nikolaus Opitz

TRANSLATION
Elise Feiersinger

PROOFREADING
Charlotte Eckler

GRAPHIC DESIGN
Willi Schmid

IMAGE EDITING
Markus Wörgötter

PRINTING
Gugler GmbH, Melk, Austria

COVER MATERIAL
Bamberger Kaliko Record

PAPER
PhoenixMotion Xenon 115g and Olin 80g

FONT
Agipo (www.radimpesko.com)

First published in German
in conjunction with the exhibition
"Martin & Werner Feiersinger: Italomodern
Architektur in Oberitalien 1946–1976,"
shown at *aut. architektur und tirol*
in Innsbruck (2012).

Park Books AG
Niederdorfstrasse 54
8001 Zurich
Switzerland
www.park-books.com

Printed on acid-free, chlorine-free paper

ISBN 978-3-03860-028-2